Jean-Jacques Friboulet, Anatole Niaméogo, Valérie Liechti, Claude Dalbera and Patrice Meyer-Bisch

Measuring the Right to Education

Contact addresses:

Interdisciplinary Institute for Ethics and Human Rights
UNESCO Chair of Human Rights and Democracy
Université de Fribourg
Rue St-Michel 6 / 1700 Fribourg / Suisse
Tél: +41 (0)26 300 73 44
Fax: +41 (0)26 300 97 07
www.unifr.ch/iiedh
iiedh@unifr.ch

Association for the Promotion of Non-Formal Education in Burkina Faso (APENF)
ADEA Working Group on Non-Formal Education
Literacy / training programme of the Cooperation Office, Swiss Embassy
01 BP 578 Ouagadougou / 01 Burkina Faso
Tél: +226 50 31 31 77
Fax: +226 50 31 88 29
aniameogo@crsbf.org

UNESCO Institute for Lifelong Learning (UIL)
Feldbrunnenstr. 58 / 20148 Hamburg / Germany
Tel: +49 (0)40 44 80 410
Fax: +49 (0)40 410 7723
uil@unesco.org

Measuring the Right to Education

Edited by
Jean-Jacques Friboulet
Anatole Niaméogo
Valérie Liechti
Claude Dalbera
Patrice Meyer-Bisch

Translated by Joanna Bourke-Martignoni

UNESCO Institute
for Lifelong Learning

Schulthess § 2006

Publication subsidised by the Board of the University of Fribourg and
the Swiss Development Cooperation (SDC)

Bibliographic information published by ‹Die Deutsche Bibliothek›
Die Deutsche Bibliothek lists this publication in the Deutsche Nationalbibliografie; detailed bibliographic data are available on the Internet at ‹http://dnb.ddb.de›.

ISBN 978-3-7255-5252-8

www.schulthess.com

Co-published in 2006 by the UNESCO Institute for Lifelong Learning
Feldbrunnenstraße 58, 20148 Hamburg, Germany

ISBN: 92-820-1150-X

ACKNOWLEDGEMENTS

The research and pilot group would like to thank all those who have contributed to this project and who have provided their ongoing support:

Koumba Boly Barry
Coordinator of the Literacy and Training Programme, Swiss Development Cooperation Office in Burkina Faso, Ouagadougou;

Serge Chappatte
Deputy Director of Swiss Development Cooperation (SDC), Head of the Development Policy and Multilateral Cooperation Division, Swiss Development Cooperation (SDC), Bern;

Jean-Maurice Delèze
Formerly Head of the West Africa section, SDC, Bern;

Etienne Dollfus
Formerly Deputy Head of the Swiss Development Cooperation Office in Burkina Faso, Ouagadougou;

Pascal Fellay
Programme Manager for the West Africa section, Project manager for the research project on measuring the right to education in Burkina Faso, SDC, Bern;

Chrystel Ferret-Balmer
Head of the Swiss Development Cooperation Office in Burkina Faso, Ouagadougou;

Catherine Graf
Head of the Statistics Unit, Development Policy and Multilateral Cooperation, SDC, Bern;

Jean-Robert Moret
Swiss Representative at the United Nations in New York, formerly Head of the Swiss Development Cooperation Office in Burkina Faso;

R. Matthieu Ouédraogo
Ex-Minister for Basic Education and Literacy (MEBA) of Burkina Faso, Ouagadougou;

Paul Taryam Illboudo
Respresentative of Swiss Workers' Aid (OSEO) in Burkina Faso at Ouagadougou;

Alice Tiendrébéogo
Director of the Fund for literacy and non-formal education (FONAENF) and the Forum for African Women Educationalists (FAWE) in Ouagadougou.

The group would like to express its most sincere gratitude to the Direction des Etudes et de la Planification (Directorate for Studies and Planning) of the MEBA (Ministry for Basic Education and Literacy), to the Directions Provinciales de l'Enseignement de Base et de l'Alphabétisation (DPEBA – Provincial Directorates for Basic Education and Literacy) and to those organisations that have provided documentation for the indicators, in particular the Oeuvre Suisse d'Entraide Ouvrière (OSEO – Swiss Workers' Aid Society), the Association Tin Tua at Fada N'Gourma, the associations Manegdbzanga and Wend Panga at Nomgana, Sahel Alpha at Gorom Gorom, Aide à l'enfance Canada (AEC – Canadian Children's Aid) at Banfora, the Association MUNYU at Banfora and the Association TON at Niangologo, and the various parents' associations, associations of mothers of students and management committees (coges) of literacy centres who were approached to assist with the study, the Direction Régionale de l'Enseignement de Base et de l'Alphabétisation (DREBA – Regional Directorate for Basic Education and Literacy) at Cascades, the Directions Provinciales de l'Enseignement de Base et de l'Alphabétisation (DPEBA – Provincial Directorates for Basic Education and Literacy) of Comoé, Léraba, Tapoa, Gourma, Oubritenga, Oudalan. The group would like to express its particular thanks to Mr. Salif Ouédraogo Director of Basic Education and Literacy for the Province of Sanmatenga, who sadly passed away prior to the publication of this book.

This research would not have been possible without the continued support of the Association for the Development of Education in Africa (ADEA) and its former president Mr Jean-Marie Byll-Cataria, programme manager in the West Africa Section, SDC, Bern. Their assistance led to the creation and development of a partnership between the IIEDHR in Fribourg and the APENF in Ouagadougou.

PILOT AND RESEARCH GROUP

Koumba Boly-Barry
Historian, Literacy and training programme, Swiss Development Cooperation Office

Maxime Compaoré
Historian, Institut des sciences des sociétés (INSS – Institute for social sciences)

Claude Dalbera
Economist – specialist in education and development, Education programme, French Development Cooperation

Jean-Jacques Friboulet
Economist, Interdisciplinary Institute for Ethics and Human Rights (IIEHR), University of Fribourg, Switzerland

Idrissa Kaboré
Geographer-demographer, Institut national de la statistique et de la démographie (INSD – National Institute for Statistics and Demography)

Jacques Ki
Educational Planner, Fund for literacy and non-formal education (FONAENF), Secrétariat permanent du Plan Décennal de Développement de l'Education de Base (SP/PDDEB, Permanent Secretariat of the Plan for the Decade of the Development of Basic Education, until the end of 2003)

Thierry Lairez
Statistician, Education programme, French development cooperation (until 2002), currently at the UNESCO Institute for Statistics

Marie-France Lange
Sociologist, Institut de recherche pour le développement (IRD – Institute for Development Research)

Valérie Liechti
Economist, Interdisciplinary Institute for Ethics and Human Rights (IIEHR), University of Fribourg, Switzerland

Patrice Meyer-Bisch
Philosopher, Interdisciplinary Institute for Ethics and Human Rights (IIEHR), University of Fribourg, Switzerland

Anatole Niaméogo
Professor of Humanities, Association for the Promotion of Non-Formal Education (APNFE), Catholic Relief Services (CRS/BF)

Adama Ouédraogo
Social psychologist, Education Programme, Netherlands Development Cooperation (until October 2004), World Bank

Fati Ouédraogo
Educator, Education programme, Canadian Development Cooperation

Germaine Ouédraogo
Economist, Association for the Promotion of Non-Formal Education (APNFE)

Rosine Ouédraogo
Linguist, Association for the Promotion of Non-Formal Education (APNFE)

Marc Pilon
Demographer, Institut de recherche pour le développement (IRD – Institute for Development Research), Unité d'Enseignement et de Recherche en Démographie (UERD – Demographic teaching and research Unit), University of Ouagadougou

Salimata Sanou-Zerbo
Educational planner, Studies and Planning Management, Ministère de l'éducation de base et de l'alphabétisation (DEP/MEBA – Ministry for basic education and literacy)

Alice Tiendrébéogo
Historian and educational specialist, Fund for literacy and non-formal education (FONAENF) and Forum for African Women educationalists (FAWE)

G. Ouédraogo and V. Liechti were responsible for the coordination of the group. V. Liechti supervised the publication and made the final corrections to the French version of the manuscript. The English translation was carried out by Joanna Bourke Martignoni. We would like to express our deepest thanks for their work.

TABLE OF CONTENTS

FOREWORD

The right to education has long been proclaimed as a fundamental human right. It is enshrined in the charters of the United Nations and of UNESCO and in the constitutions of many countries, it is one of the main preoccupations of bilateral and multilateral development, and it has been promoted by many international meetings, such as the Education for All conference held in Jomtien in 1990, the Dakar World Education Forum of 2000 and the series of UNESCO International Conferences on Adult Education (CONFINTEA). All of this has resulted in the mobilisation of enormous resources and efforts for the advancement of education world-wide. Yet, while these endeavours have brought many great improvements, the right to education still remains an elusive one for hundreds of millions of people in the world.

The present book both helps us to understand the problem better and provides some highly practical ways of addressing it. One of the many key insights offered by the book is that it is of little use to proclaim the right to education unless it is really exercised and one can measure the degree to which it is fulfilled and which conducive factors are involved. In order to do that one needs a reliable instrument and one that takes into account the wide and complex range of conditions that affect the fufilment of the right. All too often in the past we have relied on statistics that give only an incomplete picture. As the authors of this book point out: “Statistics indicating the literacy levels of the population are not enough as a measure of the effectiveness of basic education. Education is a living thing and must be integrated into the particular environment within which it is situated. The right to education must therefore be evaluated as the sum of those links which connect people to their communities and give them a better control over their lives.”

The approach presented here, which has proved itself by being applied in Burkina Faso, offers a much more finely tuned and holistic methodology than has hitherto been available. But it is not only a tool for measurement that is provided, but also a way of getting all actors and stakeholders involved to think and work together. It also involves a democratisation of access to information, for another highly important insight of the book is that the beneficiaries of the right to education must also be actively involved in monitoring and measuring the fulfilment of the right.

The UNESCO Institute for Lifelong Learning (UIL) greatly welcomes this publication, which appears at a time when the Institute and its partners are involved in many initiatives to further the right to education and learning throughout life. UIL is, for example, collaborating in a series of regional assessments in preparation for the next CONFINTEA, to be held in 2009. It is advocating the right to education by promoting learning to live and to work, by helping to design policies and create effective tools and mechanisms for recognition, validation and accreditation of informal, non-formal and experiential learning. It is also working to strengthen capacities for monitoring and evaluating literacy and non-formal education in several African countries. The Institute is also facilitating South-South cooperation to institutionalise lifelong learning. It is coordinating, on behalf of UNESCO, a major initiative launched to implement the United Nations Literacy Decade, entitled the Literacy Initiative for Empowerment (LIFE), which is targeting the literacy and basic education needs of 35 countries with 85 per cent of the world's illiterates, countries having illiteracy rates of higher than 50 per cent or more than ten million illiterate population.

The present book and the methodology contained in it represent a landmark and a new departure in the global effort to promote the universal right to education. We are confident that it will play a significant role in making that right a reality.

Adama Ouane
Director, UNESCO Institute for Lifelong Learning, Hamburg

PREFACE

This manual is a very precise working tool that has been developed by a group of researchers, statisticians and educational specialists. It is directed at those actors working on the issue of the right to education in Burkina Faso, a field that is particularly complex and changeable. The framework proposed by this book uses a group of indicators that aim at providing a clearer and more substantial reading of the application of the right to education. The indicators have been developed in order to measure a right that is effective and not illusory, real and not virtual or merely formal.

The challenge is enormous and the stakes are high. Are statistics alone enough to guarantee credibility and scientific rigour? Or do these figures coexist – like oil on water – with the real world? Do these statistics hide the living 'forest' of development? How can one use a set of figures established by empirical evidence and proven beyond any doubt in order to guarantee the right to education – which has hitherto existed only in the letter of legal texts and in the saliva of electoral speeches – as a tangible reality?

While it is true that there cannot be science without statistics, it is nevertheless important not to confuse rates of growth with growth itself and even less with development. A lack of fever according to the thermometer does not mean, on its own, that the patient is in good health. Clearly, the value of GDP and the share that is allocated to basic education are decisive factors in the promotion of that education.

However, the proverb says that in the water there is more than the crocodile. This means that it is necessary to bring other dimensions and evidence to the analysis, if we want to really understand the situation, avoiding trickery and giving a meaning to the never-ending struggle to include the knowledge factor into the triad represented by ownership, power and personal identity.

The problem is clear. One must be rigorous in finding a solution. Problem-solving means taking up an intellectual and social challenge. How can we reduce the risk of misunderstandings, of vagueness and ambiguities? Disaggregating figures and distilling the multi-faceted points of view that are brought to light by several indicators allows one to reveal the real situation. The inconsistencies come to light. The scoreboard becomes clear. The new data emphasise a number of real problems. Decoding and deciphering lead to a clearer picture, which makes it easy to select the data and to understand the true meaning of the development of the right to education.

This analytical process begins with the statement that the right to education is a dynamic set of abilities, whose supply and demand are introduced through four fundamental requirements: acceptability, adaptability, accessibility, and adequate endowments (that is, availability). The indicators stemming from these requirements enable us to clear the air for questions related to education and gives an impetus to those actors that are jointly responsible with the State for education: the private sector and civil society.

In measuring the right to education, we sometimes come up against systemic structural and constitutional obstacles that give us the desire to permanently take the side of those who are excluded from this right.

By definition, the right to education implies the duty to educate and, as a result, the present intellectual work is a sign that is also, in some ways, a signal.

Joseph Ki-Zerbo
Historian

LIST OF ABBREVIATIONS AND ACRONYMS

ADEA	Association for the Development of Education in Africa
AEC	Aide à l'enfance Canada (Canadian Children's Aid)
AI	Alphabétisation Initial (Initial Literacy)
AME	Association des mères éducatrices (Association of mothers in education)
APE	Association des parents d'élèves (Association of parents of students)
APNFE	Association for the Promotion of Non-Formal Education in Burkina Faso
BPE	Bureau des projets d'éducation (Bureau for educational projects)
CASEM	Conseil d'administration du secteur ministériel (Ministerial sector board)
CCEB	Cadre de concertation des ONG en éducation de base (NGO associative framework on basic education)
CEB	Circonscription d'éducation de base (District for basic education)
CEBNF	Centre d'éducation de base non formelle (Centre for Non-Formal Basic Education)
CEP	Certificat d'études primaires (Certificate of Primary School Studies)
COGES	Comités de gestion des centres d'alphabétisation (Management committees for literacy centres)
CONFEMEN	Conférence des ministres de l'éducation des pays ayant le français en partage (Conference of the ministers for education from countries having French as a common language)
Const BF	Constitution du Burkina Faso (Loi n° 002/97/ADP du 27 janvier 1997) (Constitution of Burkina Faso)
CRS	Cathwel Relief Services
CSLP	Cadre stratégique de lutte contre la pauvreté (Strategic poverty-reduction framework)
DAF	Direction des affaires financières (DAF/MEBA) (Directorate for financial affairs)
DAMSE	Direction de l'allocation des moyens spécifiques aux écoles (DAMSE/MEBA) (Directorate for the allocation of specific budget to schools)
DDC	Direction du développement et de la coopération suisse (Swiss Development Cooperation)
DEC	Direction examens et concours (DEC/MEBA) (Directorate for examinations)
DEP	Direction des études et de la planification (DEP/MEBA) (Directorate for studies and planning)

DGAENF	Direction générale de l'alphabétisation et de l'éducation non formelle (General Directorate for literacy and non-formal education)
DGEB	Direction générale de l'éducation de base (DGEB/MEBA) (General Directorate for basic education)
DPEBA	Direction provinciale de l'enseignement de base et de l'alphabétisation (Provincial Directorate for basic education and literacy)
DRDP	Direction de la recherche documentaire et pédagogique (ex-IPB) (Directorate for documentary and educational research)
DREBA	Direction Régionale de l'Enseignement de Base et de l'Alphabétisation (Regional Directorate for basic education and literacy)
DRH	Direction des ressources humaines (DRH/MEBA) (Directorate for human resources)
ECOM	Community Schools
EDSBF-I/II	Enquête démographique et de santé du Burkina Faso (1993/1998-99) (Demographic and health survey for Burkina Faso)
EFA	Education for All (Éducation Pour Tous)
EP1	Enquête prioritaire sur les conditions de vie des ménages (1994-1995) (Priority survey on household living conditions)
EP2	Enquête prioritaire sur les conditions de vie des ménages (1998) (Priority survey on household living conditions)
EPT	Education Pour Tous (Education for All)
F	Formal Education System
FAWE	Forum for African Women Educationalists
FCB	Formation complémentaire de base (2e année alphabétisation) (Complementary basic training/2nd year of literacy)
FONAENF	Fund for literacy and non-formal education
FTS	Formation technique et spécifique (3e année d'alphabétisation) (Technical and specific training/3rd year of literacy)
HKI	Hellen Keller Institute
I	Instituteur (teacher)
IIEDH	Institut interdisciplinaire d'éthique et des droits de l'homme (IIEHR - Interdisciplinary Institute for Ethics and Human Rights)
INEBNF	Institut national d'éducation de base non formelle (ex-INA) (National Institute for Basic Non-Formal Education)
INSD	Institut national de la statistique et de la démographie (National Institute for Statistics and Demography)
INSS	Institut des sciences des sociétés (Institute for social sciences)
IP	Instituteur principal (Head Teacher/Principal)

IRD	Institut de recherche pour le développement (Institute for Development Research)
GAP	Groupe d'animation pédagogique (Educational Training Group)
LO 96	Loi d'orientation de l'éducation N° 013/96 (Education Law)
MBDHP	Mouvement burkinabé des droits de l'homme et des peuples (Burkinabé Movement for Human and People's Rights)
MEBA	Ministère de l'éducation de base et de l'alphabétisation (Ministry for basic education and literacy)
Mfin	Ministère des finances (Direction du budget) (Ministry of Finance – Directorate for the budget)
NF	Non-Formal Education
OSEO	Œuvre suisse d'entraide ouvrière (Swiss Workers' Aid Society)
PAM	Programme alimentaire mondiale (WFP – World Food Programme)
PASEC	Programme d'analyse des systèmes éducatifs de la CONFEMEN (Programme for the analysis of the educational systems of the CONFEMEN)
PDDEB/TDPBE	Plan Décennal de Développement de l'Education (Ten-year development plan for basic education)
PNGT	Programme national de gestion des terroirs (National Programme for Land Management)
PPTE	Pays pauvres très endettés (Heavily-indebted poor countries)
PTF	Partenaires techniques et financiers (Technical and financial partners)
RGPH 96	Recensement général de la population et de l'habitation (1996) (General census of the population and living conditions)
SDC	Swiss Development Cooperation (DDC)
SP/ONG	Secrétariat permanent des ONG (Permanent NGO Secretariat)
SP/PDDEB	Secrétariat permanent du Plan Décennal de Développement de l'Education de Base (Permanent Secretariat of the Plan for the Decade of the Development of Basic Education)
UERD	Unité d'Enseignement et de Recherche en Démographie (Demographic teaching and research unit)

INTRODUCTION

In his book, *Development as Freedom*, Amartya Sen defined development as the creation of capabilities or capacities. One of the fundamental capacities is basic education. With no access to writing, reading, and numeracy, people are unable to fight against poverty and to earn their living in the current global environment. In this perspective, the right to education cannot only be conceived of as a secondary or ancillary issue. The realisation of the right to education is a principal condition for human dignity and for development. Yet, how does one measure this reality? This book aims to respond to this question by developing a method of analysis and illustrating it through the results obtained in an African country. The methodology has been developed in partners-hip with the Interdisciplinary Institute for Ethics and Human Rights (IIEHR) at the University of Fribourg, Switzerland, and with the Association for the Promotion of Non-Formal Education (APENF) in Ouagadou-gou. This methodology is new from two points of view.

The principle underlying our methodology is the explanation and appropriation by the individuals concerned of the content of the right itself. As the task of this project is to measure the effectiveness of a human right, in order to know to what extent the population benefits from the right to edu-cation, it is essential that those people concerned are able to express themselves with respect to the quality of education. In fact the educational system is not only a public good that the State has to provide. It is also an educational relations-hip, that is, a transmission of values, knowledge and know how for which the whole population is responsible in varying degrees. The approach taken here combines the traditional data used to measure "education for all" (EFA) by UNESCO with a number of indicators that enable us to assess the capa-cities of the formal and non-formal educational systems to respond to the rights of the population, in particular through their acceptability and accessibility. Indeed, the reality of the right to basic education cannot be reduced to the allocation of adequate resources to enable all children to go to school.

It is also education for all, which means a knowledge set that is adapted and acquired by children as well as adults, that provides them with real capacities to live with dignity in society. Those readers who know the educational systems in African countries will be aware that the issues of acceptability and accessibility are fundamental. Along with the lack of resources and places in schools, inefficiency, the inappropriateness of curricula and the calendar for the school year, the low level of educational completion and the lack of interest in the huge numbers of illiterate persons are also serious problems. The first part of this book describes the methodology for a systemic and interactive observation, which forms a social system within which all the agents concerned – learners, teachers, parents, administrations, NGOs, and associations – participate or should participate actively.

In the second part of the book, a series of concerning Burkina Faso are presented. These results were gathered after several surveys that were conducted following preparatory workshops and analysis during which the working group was able to refine and gradually adapt its methodology. The choice of Burkina Faso was a result of three factors:
1) the presence of the APENF, which enabled the principal agents working in the formal and non-formal systems to be brought together; 2) the representative character of the country in comparison with the rest of the region; 3) the strong commitment of the country with regards to education for all, which has been translated into the effective implementation of a plan for the development of basic education in the early 2000s and the creation of a fund to support non-formal education.

The book presents 47 indicators, which are illustrated in a table with four sections based on four capacities: acceptability, adaptability, accessibility, and availability. The indicators are integrated into a systemic framework. They describe a system in which all the factors are interdependent from each other. Some indicators will undoubtedly interest the reader more than others. It is important to remember however, that the indicators only have meaning when they are viewed as a whole. Indeed, each indicator is associated with only one dimension of the right to education, which must be respected in its entirety through an integration of the different elements that compose the right, including: health, socio-economic capacities, geography, cultural and spiritual values.

The research presented in this book took place over a period of three years. It is the result of a collective effort that mobilised a group of more than 20 researchers from Burkina Faso, Switzerland, and France. The interdisciplinary character and the diversity of the pilot and research group guaranteed the coherence and relevance of the study. The APENF and the IIEHR hope that this research will stimulate an important discussion that includes its conceptual bases as well as its results. As a complement to the other tools that have been put to practical use within the strategic poverty-reduction framework, this study represents an important step towards the achievement of the process of education for all initiated by UNESCO.

Professor Jean-Jacques Friboulet
Director of the Interdisciplinary Institute for Ethics and Human Rights, University of Fribourg, Switzerland

Anatole Niaméogo
Coordinator of the Association for the promotion of non-formal education, working group on non-formal education, Burkina Faso

PART 1

MEASURING THE RIGHT TO EDUCATION

1. SYSTEMIC ETHICAL METHOD FOR THE EVALUATION OF A HUMAN RIGHT © IIEHR / APNFE

The method outlined below was elaborated within the framework of the research work on the indicators on the right to basic education in Burkina Faso carried out by the research and pilot group. This research project is based upon the work of the IIEHR concerning the indivisibility of cultural rights. This methodology cannot be applied unless those principles that form its ethical and systemic foundations are respected.

• **Effectiveness.** The selected right is observed not only from a programming perspective but also in order to define compulsory results. These results are defined by the effectiveness of the realisation of the right (to education, to information, to adequate food and so on).

• **The individual at the centre.** The individual – that is, the subject of the right – is at the centre: it is the effectiveness of the rights to which each individual is entitled that are observed and it is these individuals, the subjects of rights, who are asked to participate, both individually and collectively, in the evaluation of the effectiveness of the right and in its implementation as well as interpretation.

• **Capacities.** The observation of a right concerns those values associated with individual capacities and the capacity of institutions to respond to the needs of individuals. These capacities, in the spirit of the General Comments adopted by the United Nations' Committee on Economic, Social and Cultural Rights, are characterised by: acceptability, adaptability, availability, and accessibility. The indicators identified in order to observe a right constitute a systemic whole and not just a simple list.

• **Ethical continuity.** In the process of developing indicators (data collection, processing and interpretation of results), the continuity of the loop value – indicator – assessment – value is respected.

• **Indivisibility of rights.** The process of observation, while concerned with one particular human right (and not with a group of rights such as the right to development), assists in the identification of connections between different rights, thereby reinforcing the principles of indivisibility and interdependence.

• **Identification.** The primary actors in the social system affected by the effectiveness of the right are identified and respected in all their diversity whether they are public, civil, or private actors working in the formal and non-formal sectors.

• **Interaction.** The different actors participate in the observation process. This means in the definition of values and indicators and in the collection, processing, interpretation and use of the results. They are called upon to create a permanent research and pilot group.

• **The three conditions for success** are:
- A coherent conception of the right within a framework of integrated development;
- A social and political demand for education;
- Partners ready to cooperate and prepared to make a commitment for the duration of the observation within a permanent research and pilot group.

2. OBJECTIVE: AN EFFECTIVE HUMAN RIGHT

All men, women, and children have the right to education with respect for their dignity. This is a legally-recognised human right.

At the universal level

1. Everyone has the right to education. Education shall be free, at least at the elementary and fundamental level. Elementary education shall be compulsory. Technical and professional education shall be made generally available and higher education shall be equally accessible to all according to their merit.

2. Education shall be directed to the full development of human personality, and to the strengthening of respect for human rights and fundamental freedoms. It shall promote understanding, tolerance, and friendship among all nations, racial or religious groups, and shall further the activities of the United Nations for the maintenance of peace.

3. Parents have a prior right to choose the kind of education that shall be given to their children.

Universal Declaration of Human Rights
(Article 26)

At the African level

1. Every individual shall have the right to education.

2. Every individual may freely take part in the cultural life of his or her community.

3. The promotion and protection of moral and traditional

values recognised by the community shall be the duty of the State.

African Charter on Human and People's Rights
(Article 17)

At the national level in Burkina Faso

Education, teaching, training, work, social security, housing, sport, leisure, health, protection for mothers and children, assistance for elderly and socially disadvantaged persons, artistic and scientific creation, are the social and cultural rights recognised in the present Constitution, which aims to promote these rights.

Every citizen has the right to education. Public instruction is non-denominational. Private education is recognised. The law establishes the conditions governing its exercise.

Unofficial translation of Articles 18 and 27
of the Constitution of Burkina Faso

Education is a national priority. Every citizen has the right to education without discrimination on the basis of gender, social status, race, or religion.

Schooling is compulsory from the age of 6 to the age of 16.

No child shall be excluded from the educational system prior to the age of 16 insofar as the available infrastructure, human resources, and school regulations permit.

Public education is non-denominational.

The languages of education are French and the national languages.

Unofficial translation of the Loi d'orientation de l'éducation au Burkina Faso 1996 (Articles 2, 3 and 4)

Yet, many children, women, and men do not enjoy the right to education and this constitutes an infringement on their dignity as human beings. There is therefore a need for action. However, in order to act effectively, it is first necessary to observe and to understand the facts.

2.1. Introduction to the observation: every individual counts

A human being who has not been able to receive basic education is unable to fully participate in the life of the community or to develop his or her capacities. This is the reason why education for everyone and by everyone must be given the highest priority: every individual counts, including the very poor, and everyone can participate in achieving the goal of universal education.

The right to basic education is considered here as the minimum threshold that enables the exercise of liberties and other rights connected to it: the right to information, the right to health, the right to work, the right to participate in the cultural life of the community, and so on.

Since everyone has the right to the satisfaction of their "basic learning needs" as enshrined in the World Declaration (Jomtien 1990), the right to fundamental education is not confined to those "who have not received or completed the whole period of their primary education". The right to fundamental education extends to all those who have not yet satisfied their "basic learning needs".

It should be emphasized that enjoyment of the right to fundamental education is not limited by age or gender; it extends to children, youth and adults, including older persons.

Fundamental education, therefore, is an integral component of adult education and life-long learning. Because fundamental education is a right of all age groups, curricula and delivery systems must be devised that are suitable for students of all ages.

General Comment no. 13 on the Right to Education, article 13 of the International Covenant on Economic, Social and Cultural Rights

Every person counts, in two important ways:

- The value of each person is taken into account, individually and as a member of the community in which she or he lives.
- Everyone participates in the evaluation of the right as each individual is responsible not only for his or her own education but also for that of others.

2.2. Observing a human right

Statistics indicating the literacy levels of the population are not enough as a measure of the effectiveness of the right to basic education. Education is a living thing and must be integrated into the particular environment within which it is situated. The right to basic education must therefore be evaluated as the sum of those links which connect people to their communities and give them a better control over their lives.

Observing a human right

- One must first gather information from those persons whose rights have been violated and understand why this is the case.
- It is then necessary to define the real value of education and its importance for everyone.
- Finally, one needs to define common strategies so that rapid and sustainable progress can be achieved.

Many individuals, associations, and communities participate in education. However, when these efforts are not coordinated, there is a lot of wastage as well as a loss of opportunity. The objective of this project is to encourage synergies between different actors.

Everyone is affected: the concept of integrated education

Basic education concerns everybody, including those for whom access to formal education has been denied or including those who have been marginalised. This implies a common responsibility for all the different actors in the formal and non-formal educational systems. Non-formal education is recognised. It includes all forms of education and learning activities structured and organised outside the framework of compulsory schooling[1].

Educational system

The "educational system" that we seek to describe is the set of relations between all actors concerned that enable an effective realisation of the right to education. It is a system of relations for which everybody is responsible and that is guaranteed by the State

This kind of system cannot be regarded as effective unless it integrates a number of very different aspects, having cultural, environmental, economic, political, and technical dimensions. For this reason, we can evaluate the educational system by measuring its capacities:

Four capacities

- Is the educational system accepted by the populations concerned: are they in agreement with the form of education?
- Is it adaptable to the different needs and circumstances of

1 Education Law (Loi d'Orientation de l'éducation du Burkina Faso, 1996)

students and learners?
- Is it available – in terms of human resources and equipment – in a way that corresponds to real needs?
- Is it accessible to all?[2]

2.3. Measuring a human right, why use a set of indicators?

The goal of this project is to measure the four capacities stated above in order to strengthen them. These capacities are those of individuals as well as those of the system as a whole and their ability to respond to the needs and fundamental rights of people.

A system of indicators

A single indicator cannot evaluate the different dimensions of education. A system forms a coherent whole that makes sense of the measure and respects the balance between individual data and institutional data, between qualitative and quantitative information, and between data from formal and non-formal systems.

While statistics are purely descriptive, the indicators have been elaborated on the ground of a referential standard. These indicators represent complex data. They also allow for chronological/historical and spatial comparisons. The indicators on the right to education are built with respect to the values established by the actors as regards the four capacities listed above.

The elaboration and design of indicators should not be reduced to a simple assessment of the educational system. They should measure the true expectations and needs of the actors involved, resulting in a greater effectiveness of the

[2] General Comment no. 13 on the Right to Education, article 13 of the International Covenant on Economic, Social and Cultural Rights, November 1999, Geneva

right to education for all. In this regard, the indicators must evaluate the quality of the educational system and be applicable to all actors.

A pilot group

The goal of this observation is to act in order to achieve a more effective right to education. This study will only have an impact if a research and pilot group is formed to learn from the observations in order to come up with solutions through collaborative efforts.

The pilot and research group is made up of people with different backgrounds. The group reflects the synergy between the different actors, both internal and external, that make up the system of basic education in Burkina Faso. It also points to the existence of a constructive dialogue between researchers and actors working in the field. The research and pilot group conceived, designed, and developed the indicators in the scoreboard that follows.

3. THE EFFECTIVENESS OF THE RIGHT TO EDUCATION: A 'WEB' OF CAPACITIES

• A right is effective when its underlying values are appropriate, observable, and verified

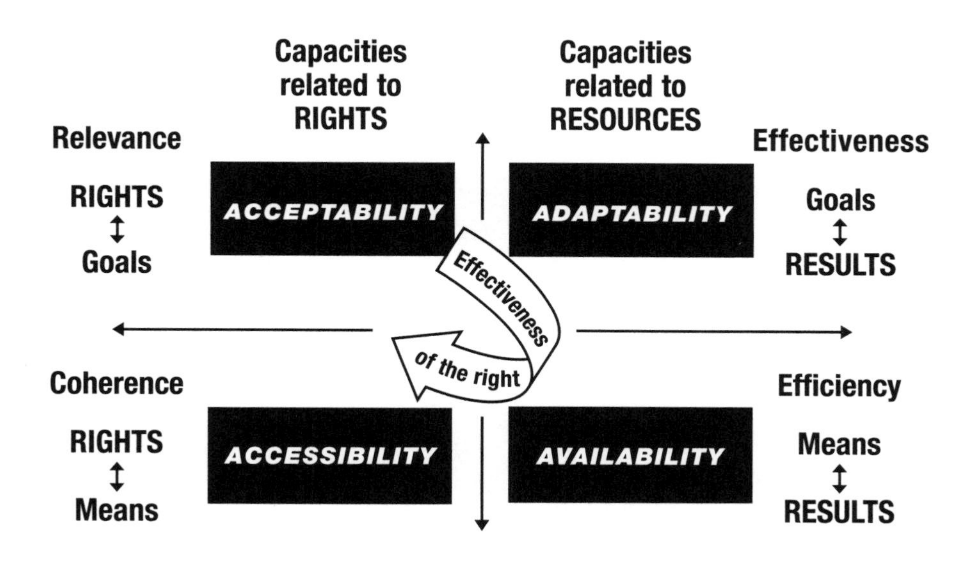

• The capacities can only be developed through a process of interaction: the capacities of the educational system connect those of individuals with the capacities of institutions.

4. ACCEPTABILITY

	VALUES to observe
Acceptability means the democratic legitimacy: the relevance of the right to education as a human right. It is the appropriation of values that the actors must constantly verify and develop within a public space in which they can all participate. In which ways does the educational system contribute to the full development of human dignity and respect for the fundamental rights of the person? Which aspects of the form and content of education provide individuals with the capacity to play a useful role in a democratic society? Do the structure and working of the system incorporating its institutions, associations, communities, and individuals respond to the real needs of each of these groups?	**Appropriation of the right** **Participation** **Exercise of freedoms within a framework of diversity**

5. ADAPTABILITY

	VALUES to observe
Adaptability is the correlation between goals and results. It is this link that defines the efficiency of the system. This correlation has four values: commitment by the actors involved, diversity of the system, awareness of the results obtained, and circulation of adequate information. Adaptability can also be directly measured by the acquisition of real capacities by the learners (which would mean that the educational system works adequately). This involves considering the needs of learners in defining syllabi, the existence of diverse educational structures, and the circulation of adequate information amongst the population.	**Commitment** **Diversity of the system** **Awareness of results** **Circulation of adequate information**

6. AVAILABILITY

	VALUES to observe
Availability puts an emphasis on the diversity of human and non-human resources in order to identify when these resources are available: this means the interaction between and capacities of people and institutions to gather the various resources that are necessary. The variety, the quality, the volume of available resources and their efficient use define the efficiency of the educational system. Human resources are multi-faceted and are not confined to learners, teachers, and trainers, but also include parents, families and communities that are called upon to collaborate. Availability of resources concerns first of all the health and nutrition status of learners as this is what affects their access to school or literacy centres as well as their capacity to learn. Next, the availability of resources relates to the training and working conditions of teachers and trainers. Finally, it is important to achieve a balance between human and non-human resources.	**Human resources** **Non-human resources (material, financial, etc.)**

7. ACCESSIBILITY

	VALUES to observe
Accessibility indicates the real availability of resources with respect to the different situations of learners. This criterion correlates the means with the rights, and makes these two elements coherent. We may describe the following dimensions of accessibility: • social and cultural accessibility: guaranteeing access to education to all persons whatever their social condition or cultural identity; • geographic accessibility: obstacles related to distance must be taken into account; • economic accessibility: both the actual costs of education and the loss of opportunities (earnings) must be taken into account.	**Non-discrimination according to:** • **gender** • **social or cultural origin** • **geographic location** • **economic status**

8. THE TRANSITION FROM CAPACITIES TO INDICATORS

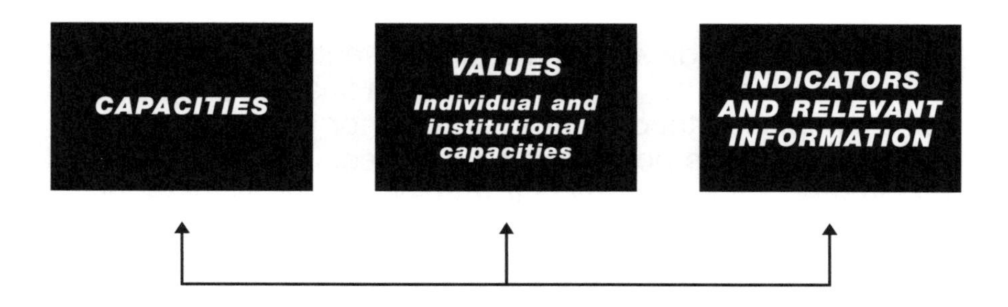

• VALUES
Individual and institutional capacities

The scoreboard focuses on people (as subjects, beneficiaries, and actors responsible for the realisation of the right) and on those institutions that are there to serve these people. The values represent the transformation of the right to education into a concrete form by all different actors. While these values are interrelated in a number of ways, they nevertheless remain distinct from each other. One value cannot be substituted for another.

The values used in the study define:

- The capacities of people to put into practice all their human rights through implementation of the right to basic education. The capacities are both the ends and the means: they are freedoms in themselves, but also resources to enable these freedoms to be realised;

- The capacities of the institutions that have been set up and developed to reach this goal.

• INDICATORS AND RELEVANT INFORMATION

Relevant information concerning the evaluation of the right to basic education cannot be summarised using a set of figures. This information also involves the use of qualitative indicators on the existence or absence of resources, and on the evaluation of the actors involved in the use of these resources in light of the goals defined.

The proposed indicators form a coherent, systemic whole. The indicators must assist in the identification of strategies for the implementation of the law, and for the optimal use of human as well as non-human resources. They must always be situated within a particular framework and within a given timeframe. The interpretation of the indicators as values must be readily accessible to all those actors using the scoreboard.

9. SCOREBOARD ON THE RIGHT TO EDUCATION

	VALUES	INDICATORS AND RELEVANT INFORMATION
ACCEPTABILITY	**1/ Appropriation of the right** Definition of values and goals, clarity and respect for institutional rules with regard to the right to education	**1/**a) Is the right to basic education enshrined in the Constitution? (1/4)[1] b) Is the right to basic education integrated into the legal bases of the different components of the educational system? (1/4) c) Do appeals mechanisms exist with respect to the implementation of the right? (1/4) d) Are the right and its different elements taken into account in the PDDEB[2]? (1/4)
	2/ Participation in the definition and implementation of policies Recognition of the diversity of actors and of the need for their intervention and interaction	**2.1** Share of government-funded public expenditure on basic education with respect to GDP (gross domestic product) **2.2** Share of public expenditure on basic education financed by foreign public funds[3] with respect to GDP **2.3** Share of public expenditure on basic education financed by foreign private funds with respect to GDP **2.4** Existence or absence of functional structures for cooperation and coordination between actors **2.5** Does the follow-up and implementation of the PDDEB involve the participation of all actors?

ACCEPTABILITY		**2.6** Existence or absence of functional assessment structures for public policies in the field of basic education **2.7** Percentage of schools with an active association of parents
	3/ Practice of freedoms in cultural and social diversity • Freedom of choice of educational establishment, language, religion • Rights of children and learners • Academic freedom • Relevance, openness and balance of school syllabi	**3.1** Percentage of schools where national languages are integrated into the teaching programme[4] **3.2** Percentage of schooling occurring in recognised private schools **3.3** Percentage of literacy centres that include income-generating activities for learners **3.4** Percentage of schools with a first-aid kit **3.5** Existence or absence of a functional framework for interpreting the degree of satisfaction[5] of learners, teachers, and parents

1 The weighting suggested for this indicator is in line with the most recent assessment of EFA carried out by the UNESCO, which considers planning at the national level as a crucial element in the definition of appropriate strategies for development and reform.
2 Ten-year development plan for basic education (TDPBE)/ Plan Décennal de Développement de l'Education de Base.
3 NGOs, decentralised cooperation, mentoring/partnerships.
4 Satellite schools and bilingual schools.
5 With respect to the functioning, values, and results of the system.

ADAPTABILITY	VALUES	INDICATORS AND RELEVANT INFORMATION
	1/ Commitment by the agents (learners, teachers, and institutions) Ability to spend the funds granted by the public sector (national and foreign)	**1.1** Number of school-aged children (7 to 12 years old) per teacher **1.2** Average number of actual teaching hours per year **1.3** Percentage of funds affected by the PDDEB that are actually spent
	2/ Diversity of the system • Variety of study fields • Integration opportunities • Skills promotion	**2.1** Percentage of learners enrolled in innovative forms of education[6] **2.2** Percentage of pupils schooled in multi-level classrooms **2.3** Number of learners enrolled in evening classes **2.4** Share of children aged between 10 and 12 who have never been to school

ADAPTABILITY	**3/ Awareness of results** • Internal and external effectiveness • Evolution • Outcomes	**3.1** Abandonment rate (F)[7] and drop-out rate (NF)[8] **3.2** Test of CM1 mathematics and French skills (F) and degree of basic knowledge (NF) **3.3** Literacy of the population aged 10+ not currently or never being schooled **3.4** Evolution of GER[9] with respect to GIR[10] **3.5** Examination pass rate (primary school certificate or literacy certificate) **3.6** Primary school completion rate by gender
	4/ Circulation of adequate information	**4.1** Number of radio stations including basic education in their programming **4.2** Percentage of literacy centres that organise reading or writing clubs

6 Centre for non-formal basic education (CEBNF), satellite schools, Banma Nuara centres (Association Tin Tua), youth centres, bilingual schools, ECOM (community schools).
7 Measures the percentage of exclusion from the primary school cycle of the formal education system (F).
8 Measures the percentage of failure and abandonment for each of the two years of training (Ai and FCB) of the system of non-formal basic education (NF).
9 Gross Enrolment Ratio.
10 Gross Intake Rate.

AVAILABILITY

VALUES	INDICATORS AND RELEVANT INFORMATION
1/ Human resources • Learners • Teachers • Trainers • Inspectors	**1.1** Percentage of malnourished children by age cohort (proxy indicator of the health status for children aged 4) **1.2** Net enrolment ratio for disabled and for non-disabled learners **1.3** Percentage of teachers with public-owned housing in good condition **1.4** Percentage of trained teachers in primary education [11] **1.5** **A/**Annual participation of teachers in the training group **B/**Annual participation of teachers in educational conferences **C/**Annual participation of teachers in other forms of training **1.6** Number of schools and literacy centres with respect to educational personnel [12] (F) or supervisors (NF) **1.7** Number of classes where no teacher was available for at least two consecutive months during the year

AVAILABILITY	**2/ Non-human resources** **A/** financial: • variety • durability • conditionality **B/** infrastructures: • safe buildings • basic equipment • a literate, equipped, healthy environment • scholastic material	**2.1** Disbursement degree of promised funds[13] **2.2** Equipment level of schools and literacy centres with regard to water, canteens, and toilets **2.3** Percentage of classrooms and literacy centres made from permanent materials and in good condition **2.4** Percentage of classrooms and literacy centres with the necessary equipment (blackboards, tables, desks, chairs, with and without cupboards/cabinets/trunks) **2.5** Percentage of students and learners with textbooks for reading and mathematics **2.6** Percentage of literacy centres with access to a library or documentation centre **2.7** Percentage of literacy centres with a child-minding facility

11 Percentage of primary school teachers who have received the minimum level of teacher training (pre-service) required for teaching: *certificat élémentaire d'aptitude pédagogique* or its equivalent.
12 Head Teacher/Principal (IP), inspectors, and educational advisors.
13 PDDEB/TDPBE.

ACCESSIBILITY	VALUES		INDICATORS AND RELEVANT INFORMATION
	Non-discrimination Measures to prevent discrimination and facilitate equality of opportunity: • at entry-level • internal • external	**1.1 Social and cultural**	**1.1.1** Percentage of women teachers and trainers **1.1.2** Female to male net primary enrolment ratio **1.1.3** Female to male drop-out (NF) and abandonment (F) rate [14]
		1.2 Geographic	**1.2.1** Number of 2nd year basic literacy training centres (FCB) [15] with respect to the number of 1st year basic literacy training centres (AI) [16] **1.2.2** Annual growth of the enrolment rate in 1st (AI) and in 2nd year (FCB) literacy training **1.2.3** Percentage of the school-aged population located further than 2.5 km from a school **1.2.4** Ratio of the gross enrolment rate in the capital city with respect to the rest of the province

ACCESSIBILITY			
		1.3 Economic	**1.3.1** Net rate of schooling (TNS) according to the family situation of the child **1.3.2** Share of annual average cost of schooling with respect to total annual household expenditure[17] **1.3.3** Share of annual average cost of literacy[18] with respect to total annual household expenditure

14 This ratio measures abandonment and failure.
15 *Formation complémentaire de base* (FCB) or complementary basic training.
16 *Alphabétisation initiale* (AI) or initial literacy.
17 The average cost corresponds in this framework to the cost of schooling of a child supported by his/her household times the average number of children of school age per household. The average cost borne by households is based on the minimum package and the different contributions paid. This package may vary depending upon the local circumstances and takes into account the materials that are necessary to enable a pupil in a given class to attend the lectures under acceptable conditions for a whole year.
18 This cost includes the cost of fees borne by the learner times the number of persons per household aged 15-44 who have never been to school or are non-literate.

10. USING THE SCOREBOARD

The goal of this scoreboard is not only to provide a method for measuring the effectiveness of the right to education. The objective is also to develop a guide that includes all of the actors involved in the observation and in the application of the scoreboard at the national, regional, provincial or local government level.

Three conditions for success

- A coherent concept of the right to education within a framework of integrated development;
- The presence of social and political demand for education;
- Partners ready to collaborate and provide a long-term commitment to participate in a permanent pilot group.

A tool with three functions

- Governance: the scoreboard is an instrument for social, cultural and democratic dialogue;
- Information and warning: the scoreboard assists in the identification of wastage and dysfunctioning;
- Development and future planning: the scoreboard allows the assessment of progress as a basis for future decision-making.

PART 2

FIELD ANALYSIS AND OUTCOMES

11. METHOD OF DATA COLLECTION

• DATA PRODUCTION

Levels of observation

Before beginning data collection, the level of observation must be determined. Which is the relevant scope or level that will enable us to measure the right to education? If this right is individual, its measure implies considering all those actors who are responsible for its effectiveness. The role of these actors in defining, implementing and controlling policies in the field of basic education enables us to determine the levels of disaggregation for the selected indicators. This is particularly true for those indicators related to processes linked to the operationality and functioning of the educational system. Two levels of disaggregation may be viewed as crucial in this context: the national level related to policy planning, and the provincial level for the implementation of action plans.

The main reference documents in the field of basic education in Burkina Faso are the Law on education (*Loi d'orientation sur l'éducation* (LO, 1996)) and the Ten-year development plan for basic education (*Plan décennal de développement de l'éducation de base* (PDDEB, 2001–2010)). The Poverty Reduction Framework Strategy (CSLP, initiative PPTE – fast track), which started in 2000, is also part of the referential framework, although it should be noted that this Strategy needs to be interpreted in light of the goals established in the earlier PDDEB. Most of the data used for the follow-up of the PDDEB come from official sources established by statistical offices of those central or regional administrative units (DPEBA) that report to the Ministry for Basic Education and Literacy (see annex 2).

The country is divided into 45 provincial administrative units that are attached to departments (an average of six per province). The major source of statistical data in relation to basic education are, nevertheless, the larger districts. This situation is largely attributable to the phenomenon of under-schooling. In practice, the geographical districts that provide the major share of statistical data are those that are covered by the school inspector. This same segmentation can also be seen in training and literacy programmes in the non-formal education sector.

In order to establish indicators relating to the functioning of the educational system, one has to look at the provincial level as the main source of data. This information base collates data from each district and allows to measure the effects of policies on the targeted population. As for the indicators connected to the operation of the system, they generally relate to the framework conditions including the legal environment that defines the orientation of educational policies. Most of these indicators refer to the national level. Some of the indicators on the right to education have been developed using data from both the provincial and the national levels, this is a result of the dual objective being pursued. The first objective was to situate the specific characteristics of the province within the national context. The second objective was to illustrate the way in which disaggregated data may be used in the definition and development of strategies for coordinated educational planning as well as to show how these data legitimise the actions undertaken in the field by the various actors and operators.

Finally, the choice of the relevant level of observation is not limited to the institutional dimension, as there is a risk that such a limitation would conceal those practices that do not conform to the logic of rights. In order to fulfil their role as an early warning signal in relation to dysfunction in the educational system, the indicators need to provide information about the demand for education as well as about the results of the educational system and the impact of policies upon the beneficiary population. Indeed, the "democratization" of information strengthens the correlation between supply of and demand for education and, as a result, the effectiveness of the right to education. To be effective, there is a need for all concerned actors to participate in the interpretation and in the assessment of the right to education. In addition, the four capacities (acceptability, adaptability, availability, and accessibility of the educational system) were also validated as the reference framework for the development of the indicators. These indicators put the subjects of the right; learners, those no longer being educated and non-learners, young people and adults at the centre of the analysis. The indicators are also connected to the subjects' socio-economic and political environment through the principles of equality and non-discrimination that affect the effectiveness of the right to education. Generally speaking, in order to reflect the different dimensions of the right to education, the indicators refer to non-scholastic data sources such as census data, household surveys, and specific surveys concerning living standards.

The approach:
a critical analysis of data and field interviews

The collection of data for the indicators was carried out in the Spring of 2004. Data collection took place as part of the follow-up to a series of surveys initiated in 2002, whose objective was to test, validate and disseminate the scoreboard on the right to education, which included several indicators. The first phase of data collection was launched in February 2002. This phase involved testing the key indicators relating to the four capacities of the educational system on various target groups, and defining a series of indicators based on the values and criteria thereby identified. In order to ensure the validity and representativity of the data, the preliminary surveys covered three provinces: Oubritenga (central plateau), Comoé (South-West) and Tapoa (East)[21]. A second round of interviews was carried out between February and May 2003, and included the provinces of Comoé and Tapoa[22]. This round enabled the testing of a first series of 63 indicators. In order to more adequately take into account the variety of the socio-economic and geographic conditions of the country,

21 Institut Interdisciplinaire d'Ethique et des Droits de l'Homme (IIEDH) [2003], *Mesurer un droit de l'homme? L'effectivité du droit à l'éducation II*. Enquêtes, FRIBOULET, J.-J., LIECHTI, V. (éd.), document de travail DT n° 8, IIEDH, Fribourg.

22 Institut Interdisciplinaire d'Ethique et des Droits de l'Homme (IIEDH) [2003], *Mesurer un droit de l'homme? L'effectivité du droit à l'éducation III. Premiers results et synthèse*, Liechti V. (éd.), document de travail DT n°9, IIEDH, Fribourg.

surveys were also conducted in a third province. The choice was made to include the province of Oudalan, situated in the North-East of the country. This Sahelian zone is characterised by a deficit of educational possibilities as well as by a lack of variety in the available options. The situation is compounded by serious problems of physical accessibility to schools and literacy centres. Hence, all these factors work together and cumulatively to keep this area in a state of perennial under-schooling, giving rise to the reproduction of regional inequalities and discouraging future interventions[23]. The province of Oudalan epitomizes in a particularly strong way the problem of the right to education. This province was the site of a pilot project for the elaboration of an educational map which provided an additional information source for data analysis.

The various stages of the research project have been implemented according to a specific methodology. This methodology centres around the idea that no distinction should be made between the principles of observation of the right to education and the principles related to the collection and validation of data. Indeed, both these principles should be considered on the same level as other constraints. A correct measurement of the right to education can only occur when it abides by the requirements of scientific rigour and precision that are necessary in this field. The exercise proved to be even more demanding than it might otherwise have been, owing to the fact that the research project had to be adapted to administrative and budgetary constraints, to the uncertainties involved in working in this field, as well as to the limited availability of human resources. With regard to the last point, all interviews were carried out by the personnel involved in the brainstorming process about the relevant indicators (see the research and pilot group). This rigorous commitment throughout the whole process provides solid evidence of the quality of the results obtained and a guarantee that these results will be followed up appropriately.

23 Lange M.-F., Compaoré M., in Institut Interdisciplinaire d'Ethique et des Droits de l'Homme (IIEDH) [2003], *Mesurer un droit de l'homme? L'effectivité du droit à l'éducation III. Premiers Results et synthèse*, Liechti V. (éd.), document de travail DT n°9, IIEDH, Fribourg, p. 55.

More precisely, the gathering of information was carried out following two guiding principles. The first, as mentioned above, was the choice of the relevant level of investigation. The second guiding principle was the optimal use of existing data in the various surveys. A comparison with the field data enabled us to proceed, using a bottom-up approach, with a critical analysis of information, thereby allowing a selection to be made on the basis of the degree of data accessibility and reliability. Once the selection had been made, the indicators were divided amongst the various groups of researchers and interviewers. These groups were formed according to the personal profiles of the people concerned taking into account the balance of gender. This balance is important to avoid certain biases (e.g. reluctance to provide specific information), but also to guarantee a cross-checking of the results. The surveys were systematically carried out following an interview guide that specified the kind of information being sought and the target public for its collection.

The results

After having tested and validated all those indicators considered as relevant to the right to education, the final stage of the research project consisted in informing, the scoreboard by concentrating on one province in particular. The pilot and research group decided to focus on the province of Sanmatenga, which is situated in the central northern part of the country. The capital town of the province is Kaya. The province includes eleven departments for eight administrative units: 1) Barsalogho, 2) Boussouma, 3) Korsimoro, 4) Mané, 5) Pibaoré, 6) Pissila, 7) Kaya I, 8) Kaya II. Out of the eight administrative divisions, seven are considered to be rural areas. Only Kaya I, attached to the capital town, may be considered to be a urban area. Out of the 237 schools registered in the province for the 2003-2004 school year, Kaya I had 22 schools. Kaya I was also the site of the largest number of private schools (8 out of a total of 21). It should also be noted that for the year considered, the gross enrolment ratio in the administrative unit of Kaya was 105.3% while this rate was only 27.7% for the rest of the province.

The non-formal sector included 14 operators carrying out literacy and other training programmes during the 2003 campaign. The number of these operators rose to 23 during the 2004 campaign. This increase can largely be explained by the contribution of the FONAENF, which provided support to 11 operators as compared to only three in the previous year. To enable the validation of the information collected that was not included in any of the pre-existing databases, the surveys covered a minimum sample size of 100 centres. The creation of the new services operated by the FONAENF in 2004 enabled the follow-up of these centres. The FONAENF teams were required to collect qualitative information with a dedicated questionnaire developed by the research and pilot group. As the FONAENF uses a group of operators that it pre-selects applying a fixed set of criteria, the information collected thereby could be biased. This bias, however, seems to be limited, on account of the small number of non-FONAENF operators in the province. Further, the information gathered has proved to be of great importance in constructing a database for the non-formal sector.

Finally, the information provided by the operators that were active during the campaigns in both 2003 and 2004 allows an assessment of the follow-up of activities at both the level of initial literacy (AI, 1st year) programmes and basic complementary training (FCB, 2nd year).

• INTERPRETING THE INDICATORS

As a general rule, the data validation should occur after an examination of the reliability of the information, notwithstanding any bias in the surveys. Data reliability however, does not depend only upon the conditions in which data were gathered, but also upon the way in which they are interpreted. There is a tendency to attribute a lack of reliability to the conditions in which data were produced while, in fact, analytical errors are overlooked. This analysis is essential for making sense of a complex reality that cannot simply be summarised in one figure. The interpretation of the indicators requires an awareness of the conditions in the field and of the dynamics of the rights involved. Moreover, the indicators must be correctly informed and analysed paying due attention to their meaning.

The interpretation of the indicators on the right to education proceeds following the same process as outlined above. The cornerstone of this process is a partnership between public, private, and civil-society actors, who have made an ongoing commitment to the process from the definition of the indicators to their interpretation and implementation. This participation leads to an increased awareness among the actors involved of both the relevance of the indicators and their utility. It also enables data validation. Participation in these terms leads to the strengthening of the individual and institutional capacities that assure the rigour and precision that are needed in order for the data to be considered reliable as well as to guarantee their correct interpretation. The success of this process leads to the possibility of developing policies and strategies for the implementation of the right to basic education.

In order for this to occur, the indicators refer, where possible, to pluri-annual data. This method enables those results that are purely factual to be kept up to date, and allows a closer link to be made with progress accomplished within the dynamic of capacities. When data are available, the indicators are informed annually and consider at least the last three years. If data are not available, the indicators are informed for each phase of the PDDEB. In general, the periodicity of the indicators depends on the data source specified for each indicator.

12. RESULTS

CAPACITY

Indicators and relevant information	**Results** **F:** Formal educational system **NF:** Non-formal educational system **P:** Province of Sanmatenga **N:** National **NA:** Not available	**Periodicity**	**Data Sources** **1/** Official data **2/** Educational statistics **3/** Non-scholastic statistics **4/** Surveys (n = sample size)

Comments
(meaning, production, results)

The following tables include all information relating to each of the 52 indicators on the right to education (see the scoreboard above). As far as possible, each indicator is presented on one page or, when necessary, on two pages. The top of the page is divided into four columns: the title of the indicator (1st column), its statistical result (2nd column), its periodicity (3rd column), and the data source (4th column). The bottom of the page is dedicated to comments on the indicator. The comments concern the meaning of the indicator, the data production, and the interpretation of the results. The shaded column on the left-hand side indicates the capacity to which the indicator refers.

13. INDICATORS OF ACCEPTABILITY

ACCEPTABILITY				
	1/a) Is the right to basic education enshrined in the Constitution? (1/4)	**yes**		**1/** Const BF
	b) Is the right to basic education integrated into the legal bases of the different components of the educational system? (1/4)	**yes**		**1/** LO 96
	c) Do appeals mechanisms exist with respect to the implementation of the right? (1/4)	**no**		MBDHP[1]
	d) Are the right and its different elements taken into account in the PDDEB? (1/4)	**yes**		**1/** SP/PDDEB

1 Movement for human and people's rights/Mouvement burkinabé des Droits de l'Homme et des Peuples.

ACCEPTABILITY

This indicator measures the national commitment with regard to the right to basic education[2] at the constitutional level, at the level of basic legislation, at the appellate level and at the level of sectoral policies. This indicator refers to the General Comment on Article 13 on the right to education under the International Covenant on Economic, Social and Cultural Rights that defines three types of obligations for State parties: obligations of implementation, of respect for, and protection of the right. These obligations imply at a minimum that States parties recognise each and every one of the rights in the Covenant and that they make a commitment to the progressive realisation of these rights[3].

While the right to education is recognised in the Constitution of Burkina Faso, it must be noted that this right is "promotional" and not considered to be a right that may be applied directly. It is perceived as a right that is a legitimate goal to attain for the whole nation (a "programmatic" right). Thus the legislation establishes compulsory schooling for children aged from 6 to 16 “as soon as the infrastructures, human resources and school regulations allow it”. In fact, the State can require a parent who does not wish to send her or his child to school to do so, but only where there is a school nearby. However, a guardian cannot oblige the State to provide schooling for her or his child in circumstances where there is no school or if there are no places available at school. In the same way, non-formal education is addressed to “all persons wishing to receive specific training in a non-scholastic educational structure” – it is plain that these structures must exist before there can be any right to access them. There are currently no appeal mechanisms at any level [micro (learner (s)), middle (civil society organisations, regional collectives and elements of the educational institution), macro (State)], that can require the immediate application or the guaranteed application within a given deadline of the right to education.

As a programmatic right, measuring the level of commitment to making the right to education effective involves an examination of the manner in which each of the components of this right has been taken into account in the sectoral policies of the State and its partners. The ten-year development plan for basic education

(PDDEB), which concerns access to, the quality of and the development of basic education, both formal and non-formal, is generally considered to be a serious and credible national commitment in support of the right to education for all. Nevertheless, if all of the components of the right have been taken into account in the PDDEB, in relation to the local context it is clear that there are difficulties in the implementation of plans of action and in the translation of intentions into results, which is what the other indicators in the table will measure by capacity.

2 The measure concerns the right to initial basic education that is considered to be at the core of the right to education. This minimum requirement corresponds, for the formal sector, to the official course of six years of primary school and, for the non-formal sector, to a cycle of learning that lasts two years, the minimal threshold for guaranteeing functional literacy (initial literacy (AI) and complementary basic training (FCB)). Initial basic education will only have meaning in terms of the right to education if this occurs within the context of permanent training that offers to young people and adults alike "a response to their basic learning needs (…) to survive, to develop their full capacities, to live and work in dignity (…)" and that "the scope of basic learning needs and how they should be met varies with individual countries and cultures and inevitably changes with the passage of time" (World Declaration on Education for All, Jomtien).

3 It should be be noted here that the Committee on Economic, Social and Cultural Rights, as the independent organ responsible for overseeing the application of the Covenant and created in 1985 by the Economic and Social Council (resolution 1985/17), unlike the Committee on Human Rights, does not possess the competence to receive individual complaints. The role of the Committee on Economic, Social and Cultural Rights is therefore limited to the examination of periodic State reports in conformity with the commitments made by States at the time of ratification of the Covenant.

ACCEPTABILITY

2.1 Share of government-funded public expenditure on basic education with respect to GDP (gross domestic product)	**N:** in %	Annual	**1/** DG/Budget/MFB; DG/EP **2/** DAF/MEBA

Years	**00-01**	**01-02**	**02-03**	**03-04**
F	1.81	1.87	1.89	
NF	NA	NA	NA	0.02

This indicator measures the part of national wealth devoted to the running and development of the basic educational system. It can be used therefore to assess the degree of general political will and the resulting internal financial resources available in support of the right to education. In terms of perspectives for the future, the indicator enables us to measure the capacity of the State, on the basis of the maximal possible internal effort, to guarantee education for all without relying on external funding, or if this funding proves necessary, in an adequate measure. The indicator allows us to evaluate the financial sustainability of the different scenarios for the development of basic education, providing us with information concerning the possibilities that would open up if the greatest priority was accorded to the right to education.

This indicator can only be correctly interpreted on the basis of a stable GDP growth (leaving out exceptional events that may have an impact on national production in a given year, as is sometimes the case in poor countries) and with a rigorous comparative perspective – making sure that comparisons are only made between countries that are structurally similar in terms of the components of national wealth and its calculation (the wealthier countries become, the more disposable income they have available, thereby making it easier to have a higher rate of taxation and, as a result, to allocate a larger proportion of their GDP to education by way of budget redistribution).

ACCEPTABILITY

In light of these observations, we can note that for Burkina Faso this indicator is weak (less than 2%) with respect to international standards[4]. The indicator is comparatively better than for other countries with less than 1000 US dollars of income per head (1.8% for Burkina Faso in 2000 against 1.6% for other countries in the same category[5]). In addition, Burkina Faso has progressed over the past few years (1.9% in 2003). This may be explained by the important share of the educational budget spent on basic education (58% in 2002)[6] and with respect to the State's own resources (22%[7], far above the norm, even internationally). A sustained level of political will should enable, in line with the expected growth of GDP, this progress to be continued and even accelerated in the future. In studying models for the accelerated implementation of education for all, an ad hoc group of government and other partners was able to calculate that a doubling of the GDP between 2005 and 2016 could lead to a tripling of the internal financial resources allocated to basic education. This increase is premised on the basis of a reasonable increase in fiscal pressure, thereby enabling a progressive adjustment to maintain balanced priorities in favour of different forms of education in relation to the fundamental needs of the population and the country. We can note that in the models and in accordance with the national educational policy, the proportion of the budget allocated to non-formal education is increasing more rapidly than the others, going from 0.9% of the total education budget in 2002 to 7% in 2016. This is the concretisation of the political awareness of the need to respond to the educational requirements of the whole population, at every stage of life, and particularly for those persons excluded from the formal educational system or those whose brief period spent in the formal system did not enable them to satisfy their fundamental educational needs even minimally, thereby denying them the right to education.

4 See reports by UNESCO, UNDP/PNUD or World Bank/BM: Ghana (2.25% in 2000), the median for emerging countries is 3%, for industrialised countries it is 5%.
5 World Bank, 2001, presentation of PDDEB.
6 Fast track request, models according to the indicative framework (MEBA 2002, rev. 2003, rev. 2004).
7 Fast track request, models according to the indicative framework (MEBA 2002, rev. 2003, rev. 2004).

ACCEPTABILITY

Indicator	Values	Frequency	Sources
2.2 Share of public expenditure on basic education financed by foreign public funds with respect to GDP	**N:** in %	Annual	**1/** BPE **3/** FONAENF+PTF (Luxembourg project, PNGT[8], literacy/training programme[9])

Years	**00-01**	**01-02**	**02-03**	**03-04**
F	0.32	0.73	1.26	
NF	NA	NA	0.04	0.08

This indicator measures the importance of bilateral or multilateral public development assistance (PDA) given in the form of gifts or loans conditional upon support for national policies on basic education.

In Burkina Faso, at the end of the 1990s, the volume of external aid had attained its maximal level and was stagnant. Since the adoption of the Plan for the Decade of the Development of Basic Education (PDDEB) and the creation of new instruments for mobilising and channelling development assistance ("common basket" of donors and funds for literacy and non-formal education), we can observe an important upswing in external commitments in favour of basic education, both formal and non-formal. This trend has been reinforced by the favourable international context (World Forum in Dakar, Millennium Summit in 2000, Monterrey Consensus, Amsterdam Meeting and Kananaskis Summit in 2002, Brussels and Paris Conferences in 2003 on the accelerated financing of EFA).

The indicator, however, raises the question of the ear-marking of this assistance in the different budgets for the functioning and investment in basic education. It also raises the problem of the variability of data for these countries. The question of the longevity of these commitments has yet to be answered, despite the statements being made by international donors. The problems of administrative and financial procedures, of capacities to run programmes, of conditionalities that are mutually acceptable and of institutional changes relating to the assistance, have yet to be solved in a satisfactory and sustainable manner by the parties concerned. Finally, the international doctrine on assistance, while encouraging a greater coherence and synergy between donors in support of a national policy conceived and executed in the country itself, is still seeking a minimum of consensus surrounding the necessary balance between budgetary aid (contributions to the overall State budget), the assistance programme (contributions to sectoral budgets) and project aid (contributions to budgets targeted on the basis of micro territories and/or beneficiary public).

8 National programme for land management.
9 Swiss Development Cooperation (DDC).

ACCEPTABILITY				
	2.3 Share of public expenditure on basic education financed by foreign private funds with respect to GDP	NA	At each stage of the PDDEB	**1/** SP/ONG **3/** CCEB

This indicator seeks to measure the importance of international non-governmental cooperation in favour of education for all. Unfortunately, it is very difficult to produce a reliable indicator as, on the one hand, civil society organisations are increasingly being financed with public funds in addition to their own private funding sources and, on the other hand, with respect this private financing, it is very difficult to differentiate those funds that may be accounted for by year and by exact destination (here, basic education, both formal and non-formal).

In addition, the available figures only take into account the contribution of those NGOs and partnerships that have some visibility, are of a relatively large scale, and are willing to participate in data collection. These figures are not exhaustive and under-estimate the contribution of international solidarity among citizens. There are, however, ways and means of improving these statistics (through annual statistical surveys at the provincial level, and a national day of statistics (on education and economy)). The cooperation service in the DEP/MEBA is currently elaborating a tool that should enable the construction of statistics on education in order to better inform this indicator.

In the meantime, we can move forward empirically, with the certainty that the share of external non-governmental financing with respect to non-formal education is much higher than for formal education, while the formal education sector is increasingly being funded owing to the success of the world campaign in favour of education for all.

ACCEPTABILITY

2.4 Existence or absence of functional structures for cooperation and coordination between actors	**Year 2004** | **Provincial**	**National** **F**	yes	yes **NF**	yes	yes	At each phase of the PDDEB	**2/** DPEBA

This indicator points to the existence or not of organised frameworks for enabling the association and coordination of all stakeholders. The existence of functioning structures is a fundamental requirement for the participation of all actors. The indicator is assessed differently at the national and provincial levels and for the formal and non-formal education sectors[10].

This indicator and the following two are indicators of the operationality and coherence of the system. The triad of indicators brings to light a crucial element of the definition of strategies, the implementation and the evaluation of policies as regards education, namely tripartite partnerships between public, civil society and private actors. The indicator also relates to the question of the real participation of these actors and their representativeness. The quality of the partnership requires that the actors have not been instrumentalised by the State as simple sub-contractors. The degree of interaction between the actors is, in fact, the first index of the optimal performance of a system. The level of interaction means that the institutions are not prisoners of

10 For indicators 2.4-2.5-2.6, a distinction is made between the national and provincial levels:
National: Structures for coordination and functional cooperation for the formal and non-formal sectors are: CSLP (cadre stratégique de lutte contre la pauvreté/strategic framework for poverty reduction), CASEM (conseil d'administration du secteur ministériel/board for the ministerial sector), Mid-term reviews of the PDDEB (joint missions), Final reviews, National balance sheet (NF)
Provincial: Reviews by phase of the PDDEB, Regional and provincial systematic assessments (NF).

their pre-programmed functions, and that they adapt and complement each other through various mechanisms according to the strengths and weaknesses of each, thereby assuming a common responsibility[11]. The involvement of the various actors is also underlined in the assessment report on EFA by the UNESCO. The commitment by civil society, in particular, is considered to be the basis of sustainable planning for education[12].

11 Patrice Meyer-Bisch in DT n° 7 IIEDH, *Mesurer un droit de l'homme? L'effectivité du droit à l'éducation I, Enjeux et méthodes*, avril-mai 2003, p. 17.
12 UNESCO [2002] "Education pour tous. Le monde est-il sur la bonne voie?", Rapport mondial de suivi sur l'éducation pour tous, Ed. UNESCO, France, p. 120.

ACCEPTABILITY				
	2.5 Does the follow-up and implementation of the PDDEB involve the participation of all actors	**2003-2004** **P:** Only for some actors	At each stage of the PDDEB	**2/** DPEBA
	This indicator checks, at different levels and for the formal as well as for the non-formal educational sector, if the actors have been requested to contribute to a global follow-up of the programme within which their particular activities are occurring (over and above the issues related to the implementation of their own programmes). When provincial programmes are set up, it may be appropriate to give the highest priority to strategies and the creation of activities. The national experience of joint follow-up and implementation missions for the PDDEB has shown that a large participation, even when regulated and only including one representative per actor category and two or three representatives for each "key" actor category, can rapidly lead to missions of 150 to 250 persons. This causes specific problems relating to the organisation of the work to be done and the quality of the follow-up that have yet to be resolved.			

ACCEPTABILITY				
	2.6 Existence or absence of functional assessment structures for public policies in the field of basic education	**2003-2004** **P:** yes **N:** yes	At each stage of the PDDEB	**2/** DPEBA

This indicator observes, at different levels and for the formal as well as for the non-formal, the existence or lack of functional mechanisms for evaluation, that is to say, producers of adequate data and analyses that would enable an assessment of public policies in relation to basic education based on their results and their impact. It therefore measures the importance accorded to the evaluation of policies in order to increase their relevance.

Over and above the problem of partnerships, which is always crucial, this indicator has the role of bringing to light another essential aspect of the definition of strategies, implementation, follow-up and evaluation of educational policies, that is to say the provision of reliable and recognised data and the contribution of research to the development of operational analysis.

Concerning the different actors involved, we can observe that the dominant trend in relation to evaluation is to turn to large consultancy firms. We can ask questions about the relevance of these practices in relation to the consequences of the use of large external consultants to conduct evaluations: low level of acceptability and ownership, artificial nature of the participation of other actors, the fact that this perpetuates a low standard of research at the local level, the suitability and level of adaptation are questionable, high level of cost involved.

In relation to the data, the problems, largely administrative, stem in the main from difficulties related to the treatment and non-use of results.

An independent and multi-actor observatory on education constitutes an adequate solution to the above-mentioned difficulties. A proposal in this regard has already been made and is still being evaluated.

ACCEPTABILITY

2.7 Percentage of schools with an active association of parents	**2002-2003** **P:** 33.5%	Annual	**2/** DEP/MEBA

This indicator allows for an assessment of the degree of involvement of parents and communities in the evolution of institutions. It provides information on the openness to participation in the system dynamics.

An "active" parents association means an association that carries out at least one activity other than those duties that are formally required of it (checking of presences and material contributions to the running costs of the school). These associations contribute in one way or another to what may be called the "school project", that is, a set of teaching, leisure, practical, cultural and other activities designed and carried out by the school in interaction with its environment.

Note that this indicator depends on statement-based data. The problem of the linkages between "school-environment" and "parents-teachers" is particularly complex. It is likely, for example, that some associations were considered "inactive" because they were openly or covertly in conflict with the teaching staff who sometimes reject what they consider as an intrusion by parents, or because the association itself has not been able to assert itself owing to a leadership problem. It should be observed that it is often those "inactive" prominent individuals who hold positions on the board or as representatives of parents associations and that this can hide the real but circumspect activities being undertaken by other members of the association.

ACCEPTABILITY

Indicator	F: in %				Periodicity	Sources
3.1 Percentage of schools where national languages are integrated into teaching programme	Years	**01-02**	**02-03**	**03-04**	Annual	**2/** DEP, DGEB/MEBA DPEBA **3/** OSEO[13], PAM[14]
	P	9.9	9.3	9.1		
	N	4.9	5.0	5.6		

This indicator measures the capacity of the educational system to provide a school that is adapted to the socio-cultural environment in which the population lives and, therefore, is more acceptable to these individuals. This indicator raises the issue of the languages of instruction for basic education. The indicator must be interpreted in light of the historical and political context of a given country. In the case of former-colonies, the official language is generally promoted exclusively as a factor of national integration, openness towards the rest of the world, and access to modernisation, while national languages are stigmatised as dividing and isolating factors, and as responsible for keeping the country in a state of under-development, in spite of the fact that these national languages are spoken by the majority of the local population.

In Burkina Faso, the share of bilingual schools is still small, which shows that the issue of education in national languages has yet to be resolved. The evolution of this indicator is particularly interesting with regard to the increasing effectiveness of the right to education through the creation of an acceptable supply of education.

13 Oeuvre suisse d'entraide ouvrière/Swiss Workers' Aid Society.
14 All satellite schools receive WFP aid.

ACCEPTABILITY

Indicator	Data	Frequency	Source
3.2 Percentage of schooling occurring in recognised private schools	**F:** in %	Annual	**2/** DEP/MEBA

Years	**00-01**	**01-02**	**02-03**
P	5.5	7.6	8.4
N	8.1	8.7	9.1

This indicator measures the portion of private schools in the formal education system. The existence of private schools strengthens the variety of the supply of education, a necessary condition for the effectiveness of the right to education. This is a key aspect of cultural diversity at the same level as linguistic pluralism. Cultural tolerance is based on religious tolerance as much as it is on linguistic tolerance[15].

To interpret this indicator, it is important to take into account the socio-historical context of the school system, as the criteria for the recognition and financing of different types of denominational schools may vary over time. In addition, it should be noted that the evolution of the number of students is not a true gauge of an improvement in choice or of free access to a diversified supply. The number of students attending school may actually hide inequalities of treatment with respect to access (enrolment fees). For this reason, the indicator must be assessed by taking into account the policies of public subsidies for private teaching. In Burkina Faso, this sector is little developed and one can assume that the number of private schools will not increase above 10% owing to the high financial costs of access to these schools for poor households. Despite its limitations, this indicator nevertheless raises the question of the expectations and needs of some members of the population with respect to education.

15 UNESCO [2003], "Déclaration universelle sur la diversité culturelle", Série diversité culturelle n°1, éd. UNESCO, Paris, p. 4 and p. 57.

ACCEPTABILITY

3.3 Percentage of literacy centres that include income-generating activities for learners	2003-2004 **P:** 28.2 %	Annual	**2/** DPEBA **4/** Sanmatenga n = 245 centres

This indicator measures the share of literacy centres that, in conformity with the national consensus, effectively link the development of basic knowledge with the production of income-generating goods or services. According to this doctrinal consensus, basic education is not an end in itself but may be situated within the actual dynamics of local development, in particular economic development. The indicator is not easy to inform, given the extreme variety of situations in the field and the different methods of including these activities within the indicator.

This indicator was chosen as a result of the importance given by learners, in particular female learners, to the existence of income-generating activities. The field surveys showed that the level of attendance at literacy centres was heavily dependent on the consideration given to lost income for those people who were working. It seems that the real cost of access to the programmes (enrolment fees and cost of equipment)[16] is less likely to be an impediment to adult literacy than the loss of earnings engendered by the giving-up of an income-generating activity (rural activities, small businesses) and/or social factors, in particular for women (care for family members, activities and constraints due to family, housework).

16 Concerning Burkina Faso, enrolment fees for literacy programmes do not exceed 3,650 Fcfa per year and per learner.

ACCEPTABILITY

3.4 Percentage of schools with a first-aid kit	NA	Annual	**2/** DEP/MEBA, DPEBA, DAMSE[17] **3/** CRS[18], FDC[19], HKI

This indicator measures the degree of involvement of the school in the provision of basic medical care for students. The indicator highlights the relationship between the child and her/his rights. Generally speaking, the indicator reveals the way in which the institution, teachers, parents and students view the school as a place for living and socialising (leisure activities and security). If we perceive the school as a place where the child can receive an initial response to those fundamental rights that are not taken into account elsewhere (for instance, the right to education but also the rights to health, food, and culture), the indicator can be seen as particularly relevant.

The figures concerning Burkina Faso are not currently available. However, the data should be collected in the long term by the DEP/MEBA through the use of statistical survey files.

17 Direction de l'allocation des moyens spécifiques aux écoles/Directorate for the allocation of specific budget to schools.
18 Cathwel Relief Services.
19 Foundation for community development.

ACCEPTABILITY

3.5 Existence or absence of a functional framework for interpreting the degree of satisfaction of learners, teachers, and parents	**2003-2004** | **Province** **F** | no **NF** | yes	At each stage of the PDDEB	**2/** DPEBA

This indicator measures the existence of a functioning framework for the expression of satisfaction by learners, teachers, and parents at different levels. The framework is aimed at identifying the demands of individuals rather than those of interest groups (unions, parents associations). Considering this element seems to be fundamental in terms of the right to education. The interpretation of the results however is difficult owing to the methodological problems related to the formulation of the indicator.

According to the DPEBA of Sanmatenga, at the formal sector level, assessments are systematically carried out by teachers and by parents associations at the end of each school year. We can therefore, argue that there is a system of planned management for the school (for example, 50 schools came together to define an action plan). However, this process cannot be truly considered as an expression of the satisfaction of teachers and parents, because it does not take into account recurrent demands by the teachers concerning their working conditions, the issue of the school calendar for the parents, overall conditions at school for the children, and so on.

For the non-formal sector, a similar framework exists through the process of assessment and programming reports that include all these aspects (this does not mean, however, that the main critiques and demands are taken into account).

ACCEPTABILITY

The functionality of a framework for the expression of satisfaction depends on its capacity to assert its demands at the political level, in the way provided for in the PDDEB. For this reason, it is important to acknowledge these frameworks as an element of the functional system for the evaluation of basic educational policies.

14. INDICATORS OF ADAPTABILITY

Indicator	Years	01-02	02-03	03-04	Frequency	Source
1.1 Number of school-aged children (7 to 12 years old) per teacher	**P**	136	122	118	Annual	**2/** DEP/MEBA, DGEB **3/** INSD
	N	105	94	94		

This indicator measures the constraints brought to bear on the formal system and its extension in connection with the goal of primary-level schooling for all. It takes into account the number of teachers required to guarantee the process of universal primary education in the long run (taking as a reference point an acceptable ratio in terms of the goal of "one teacher for 40 children"). To assess the indicator correctly, it must be noted that this measure only counts those teachers actually employed, including relief teachers, and not the entire staff set of trained teachers available. This difference could prove to be very significant. It appears, nevertheless, that the goal of universal education for Burkina Faso cannot be met without the recruitment of a large number of teachers.

It should be noted that the equivalent indicator for the non-formal sector, that is the number of illiterate or newly-literate students per teacher, had to be omitted for practical reasons. It would have been necessary to calculate the indicator based on age cohorts (for 12-14 year olds, 15-24 year olds, 25-44 year olds, 45-59 year olds, and 60 years and older according to the categories established in General Comment no. 13 and by the UNESCO) and then evaluate the number of trainers teaching each of these groups.

ADAPTABILITY

1.2 Average number of actual teaching hours per year	**P: 2003-2004** **F:** 599 hours	Annual	**2/** DPEBA

This indicator measures the real opportunities for basic knowledge acquisition based on a minimum annual volume of teaching hours.

In Burkina Faso, the official volume of teaching hours for primary school teachers is situated between 720 hours and 1020 hours per year according to the reference base used (Education law, annual ministerial decree, local academic decision on the start of the school year).

The calculation of the number of effective teaching hours per year refers, first of all, to the dates for the start and end of the school year as these are fixed by the DPEBA for each province (these often differ from the dates set by the central administration). This period enables a determination to be made of the overall number of teaching hours[1] that serves as the basis for the calculation. This theoretical number of teaching hours is then assessed with respect to the calendar, on the one hand and, on the other hand, with respect to the school syllabus. This calculation requires data relating to each school[2].The schools themselves provide information concerning the actual dates for the start and end of the school year as well as data on classes held throughout the year; in other words, on the number of effective teaching days. The assessment of the reasons given for the cancellation of classes, only takes into consideration those teacher absences related to professional development, administration or for training.

The result therefore corresponds to the difference between the total number of non-teaching days in addition to public holidays and other official leave periods, and the total volume of teaching hours for the province.

A test survey was carried out in October 2004 in the district of Kaya I. The survey brought together the DPEBA and two school principals. The information collected showed that the theoretical volume of teaching hours for the province is 720 hours. This volume covered a period of 32 weeks from 1 October 2003 to 15 May 2004. Excluding holidays and other official days of leave, the school programme took place over 24 weeks, which is equivalent to 720 hours.

The survey revealed that 30 teaching hours were lacking owing to the failure to adhere to the school calendar by starting school one week later than planned. As for the number of non-teaching days, these were identified and broken down in the following way: 10 days[3] due to the absence of teaching for continued education (mainly GAP), 4 days for administrative tasks (development of teaching tools, exam questions etc.) and 1 day for local events or non-official holidays. Note that teacher absences for reasons such as salary collection, illness or maternity leave were not taken into account. Nevertheless, these factors could prove to be important[4].

Based on this information which may be considered to be reliable but not necessarily representative, the result can be calculated as 599 teaching hours, that is 83.2% of the total volume of 720 hours. This indicator was preferred over an indicator based on absolute figures as it provides a demonstration of the real possibilities offered to the child in order for her/him to acquire a minimum of basic knowledge. This result must be explained for at least two reasons. The first concerns the “double flow” system. In the two cases studied, the model followed by the school was what is known as the 212 (2 teachers, 1 class, 2 age cohorts). Rather than being held daily, the school programme takes place on every second day. For each age cohort the programme is reduced correspondingly. The second reason relates to the fact that the calculation does not take into account those teacher or student absences that cannot be justified.

Finally, the interpretation of this indicator raises a question of substance: the capacity of the system to offer a full educational service and to respect this through a continual adaptation taking into account the various external constraints that affect it. It is interesting to make a comparison based on scientific data of the results with those of other countries in the sub-region and with international standards (752 compulsory hours for children aged 7 to 8 years and 812 hours for children aged 9 to 11 years being the averages for OECD countries (2002)). The UNESCO report [2002] gives the median number of teaching hours for low-income countries: 667.3 hours in the 1st year and 827.8 hours in the 6th year of schooling and for high income countries: 752.9 hours in the 1st year and 845.3 hours in the 6th year).

1 Timetable based on which the different subjects are scheduled.
2 This information is available in school registers or otherwise in the teachers' lesson plan books.
3 6.5 hours of classes are counted per day.
4 These absences are particularly important in remote regions: for instance, the Provinces of Tapoa and Comoé, see DT n° 9 IIEDH.

ADAPTABILITY

1.3 Percentage of funds affected by the PDDEB that are actually spent	**N:** NA	At each stage of the PDDEB	**1/** BPE **3/** FONAENF

This indicator aims to measure the capacity of the ministry to absorb the credits allocated to it for the implementation of the PDDEB. What we are calculating here is the amount that is being paid in each quadrennial or triennial stage of the plan (whether this occurs on an annual basis or not is not relevant to the periodicity of this indicator), all funding sources (internal and external) combined.

The results are difficult to measure and must be interpreted with care as their components are very different: we can observe a high commitment level with respect to internal resources but a low commitment level in relation to external resources, which underlines a related problem of external aid adaptability.

ADAPTABILITY

<table>
<tr>
<td>2.1 Percentage of learners enrolled in innovative forms of education</td>
<td>In %:
<table>
<tr><td>Years</td><td>01-02</td><td>02-03</td><td>03-04[5]</td></tr>
<tr><td>P</td><td></td><td>5.6</td><td>5.4</td></tr>
<tr><td>N</td><td>1.9</td><td>2.1</td><td>2.7</td></tr>
</table>
</td>
<td>Annual</td>
<td>2/ DEP/MEBA
DPEBA
3/ Operators (OSEO)</td>
</tr>
</table>

This indicator measures the share of innovation in the educational sub-system with respect to the 7-15 year old cohort. The numerator here is the number or learners enrolled in innovative educational systems[6]. As regards the denominator, we included the total number of students in the formal and non-formal sectors.

The importance of this indicator lies in its ability to provide information concerning the diversification of the educational offer available to children and youth. These innovative educational projects are largely targeted at children and young people, and represent alternatives to the formal system. Emanating from the non-formal sector, these innovative programmes have a strong capacity to adapt to demand. In the long term, the indicator will provide more precise information concerning the actual demands being made by the population, that is to say, the interest that the population has in innovative educational projects. At the time of writing, the figures point to the fact that supply does not meet demand. In the favourable context of Burkina Faso, which is characterised by the implementation of the PDDEB and by the steady progress made in the number of bilingual schools, this indicator should show some positive dynamics in the future.

5 Total number of learners in the formal system: 35,447 learners; Satellites: 1,186 learners; Bilingual schools: 636 learners; CEBNF: 197 learners.

6 In Burkina Faso, these structures include centres for non-formal basic education (CEBNF), satellite schools, Banma Nuara centres (Association Tin Tua), youth centres and bilingual schools.

ADAPTABILITY

Indicator	Data	Frequency	Source
2.2 Percentage of pupils schooled in multi-level classrooms	**F: in %:**	Annual	**2/** DEP/MEBA

Years	**00-01**	**01-02**	**02-03**
P	32.6	31.1	33.4
N	18.0	18.7	19.4

This indicator measures the share of students being taught in composite classes, in light of the estimation that 70% of the population of Burkina Faso lives in remote rural areas and that it is this portion of the population that is the potential beneficiary of these initiatives. The model of a multi-level class structure is an alternative to the classic structure of six classes with six teachers which is better adapted to the urban environment[7] or to a rural setting with a large population living close together. This classic model enlarges the school catchment area thereby increasing the distances that children have to travel, which is both a factor in under-schooling and the cause of a notable deterioration in learning conditions (particularly for girls). In the multi-level class system, the school only has three classes, and each teacher is in charge of two years of the primary school cycle: CP1/CP2, CE1/CE2, CM1/CM2 (according to the model most commonly used in Burkina Faso). Note that schools using the multi-level class model with two teachers, or even with one teacher, may be established in the future in order to school children living in hamlets where there are small, isolated populations, or for children from minority groups (seasonal workers, semi-nomadic populations, and nomads in particular).

This indicator therefore represents a key indicator of adaptation in order to allow for real progress to be made towards universal education, also in areas where there is currently a large proportion of under-schooling owing to excessive distances between home and school.

The extension of multi-level classes to rural areas is one of the goals of the PDDEB as regards to the extension of access to basic education and the optimal use of human and material resources[8]. The data are reliable and accessible. A detailed analysis of progress in this area is particularly interesting from the perspective of the effectiveness of the right to education for all. Such an analysis requires additional qualitative survey work.

7 According to the INSD, in 2000 the rate of urbanisation was 16.5% in Burkina Faso.
8 PDDEB, op. cit., p. 17 and 32.

ADAPTABILITY	**2.3** Number of learners enrolled in evening classes	**P:** 2002-2003 **F:** 58 learners	Annual[9]	**2/** DPEBA

This indicator measures the opportunities for access to formal education beyond official class schedules and course syllabi for those persons who have withdrawn from schooling or who have never been to school and who have expressed their desire to access education through the appointment of voluntary teachers (paid by the students requesting this service).

Evening classes concern different student profiles: children older than 10 who have never been to school or who are not currently enrolled, young people who are failing or who have abandoned school and, finally, adults in urban areas seeking functional literacy in French. The heterogeneity of the demand gives rise to problems with respect to the content of programmes. Until recently, the phenomenon of evening classes has been little – documented. Surveys, including the one supported by Diakonia, are currently being undertaken in order to gather information with respect to this spontaneous system that offers a real “second chance” for education to many thousands of people.

This indicator provides information concerning the capacity of actors to respond to the unsatisfied educational needs of people in accordance with the commitments made at Jomtien in relation to life-long learning.

10 Taken into account in the surveys conducted by the MESSRS and MEBA.

ADAPTABILITY

Indicator	Data	Source	Reference
2.4 Share of children aged between 10 and 12 who have never been to school	**N:** 1998, in % Location | **Boys** | **Girls** | **Total** **Urban** | 16.3 | 22.7 | 19.4 **Rural** | 68.0 | 80.4 | 73.8 **BF** | 60.3 | 71.3 | 65.5	Depends on the data source	**3/** EP 98 but preferably EP 2003 (not available)

The interest of this indicator lies in the fact that it provides a measure of the number of students who have no access to school. It is an indicator of the level of exclusion from the formal system. The results indicate that approximately 7 out of 10 girls and 6 out of 10 boys were in this situation at the time of the referential survey (98). The number of students without access to school varied considerably according to place of residence: the highest figures were 16.3% in urban settings for boys and 80.4% in rural areas for girls. While the educational achievement rate falls (providing a measure of school failure), this indicator also provides a forecast, as it enables an estimate to be made of the minimal educational base required by future candidates for the non-formal system.

The lower age limit considered for the indicator is 10. This corresponds to the age at which the child can no longer claim the right to primary-level schooling. The upper age limit corresponds to the official age for the end of primary-level schooling. To better reflect the reality of the situation, the age limits used may vary according to the place of residence. The indicator largely refers to the primary school cycle, but it could also be extended to cover the whole period of compulsory schooling, which goes from 10 to 16 according to the national legislation in this field.

ADAPTABILITY

3.1 Abandonment rate (F) and drop-out rate (NF)

P:

Years	00-01	01-02	02-03	03-04
F/				
CP1	12.7	4.8	6.7	7.2
CP2	8.0	10.3	3.5	5.5
CE1	7.2	7.0	10.4	9.4
CE2	8.1	9.7	4.9	5.3
CM1	8.7	4.4	10.1	8.2
NF/				
AI		33.1	44.3	34.9
FCB		20.4	25.8	26.9

Annual

2/ DEP/MEBA DGAENF

ADAPTABILITY

This indicator enables an appraisal of the capacity of the system of basic education to realise the goals of education for all, not only in terms of initial enrolment in the system but also in connection with the retention of these pupils at each phase of the programme of basic studies.

The abandonment rates used in the formal sector are calculated by level, owing to the difficulties related to the production, use, and interpretation of the median rate of school abandonment over the whole primary school cycle (or of the attempt to establish the opposite measure, that is, the rate of school attendance). The rates for abandonment per level give us data related to those students who have been excluded from the formal system during their first five years of schooling.

The rates of progressive drop out are calculated for the non-formal sector. The difference between rates of abandonment and the calculations with respect to drop out is that the rate of drop out takes into account both abandonment and failure in the context of the basic cycle of non-formal education.

For Burkina Faso, the results are particularly significant and illustrate the extent of drop out amongst learners. The results point to the inability of the system to limit the number of drop outs through maximum adaptability. In a comparative perspective for the sub-region, which collates similar results, it should be noted that the possible reasons for the level of abandonment and drop out are many and multi-faceted. Surveys have shown that, for the most part, the reasons for abandonment or drop out are external to the system: social factors (e.g. health problems and economic survival), psychological causes (loss of self-confidence and abandonment owing to difficulties associated with learning). Yet, the system itself accentuates these phenomena by frequently rejecting those learners who fail to adapt to the system itself or to the authority of its actors (large number of programmes, inadequate behaviour of some teachers or trainers, rigid nature of the educational supply which fails to take into account some learner profiles, particularly with regard to their culture, language or gender – this often pushes learners to abandon or fail).

ADAPTABILITY

3.2 Test of CM1 mathematics and French skills (F) and degree of basic knowledge (NF)	**P: Year 2004** **F:** Test in French: 15/34[10] Test in mathematics: 18/33[11] **NF:**	At each stage of the PDDEB	**4/** Sanmatenga F: n=225 students NF: n=187 learners

Results in %	**M**	**F**	**Total**	**15-24 years**
1/ Able to express themselves in writing: production of a short text relevant to their life (literate as defined by the UNESCO)	77.0	57.0	70. 0	71.0
2/ Can write a message without omitting essential information (names of the sender and recipient, clear subject of communication) (functionally literate)	46.0	37.0	43.0	42.0
3/ Mastery of writing and adding of 3 numbers with several figures	50.0	37.0	46.5	46.0
4/ Percentage of correct responses to basic questions in history/geography/health/ agriculture	59.0	47.5	55.0	51.0

ADAPTABILITY

This indicator, originally the level of basic knowledge, seeks to provide information about the percentage of those learners who, having previously completed a full cycle of basic education still maintain a skill level that meets their fundamental educational needs. This indicator is based on the notion of fundamental educational needs as proposed by the Jomtien and Dakar conferences (reading, writing, arithmetic and general functional knowledge that enable a socio-economic and civil integration in accordance with local living conditions and their development). The information provided by this indicator reveals the extent to which the right to education has been effectively implemented for the persons concerned, in the sense of the international right to basic education for all at all times of life (according to the Covenant and General Comment no. 13).

With respect to the formal system, this kind of data was not available and so the researchers referred to PASEC tests set up for this purpose. These tests also enable the creation of points of comparison over time and space. It should be noted that the PASEC tests provide information on the level attained in the fifth year (CM1) in French and in mathematics and do not provide a real basis for the appraisal of basic student knowledge at the end of their schooling. In addition, the use of these tests often raises several questions:

- Are the CM1 level and the subjects of study relevant with regard to the information being sought?
- The content raises issues with regard to the understanding of terminology. Developed for Senegal, the test includes specific terms that do not apply to the situation in Burkina Faso (for instance *la calèche*).
- The conditions surrounding the administration of the test can also give rise to important biases in the interpretation of the results. The choice of the person in charge of supervising the test as well as the time of day when the test is taken (morning or afternoon) can have a considerable influence on the results.

With these caveats in place, it can be seen that the percentage of students in the fifth year of the formal system with fundamental elementary knowledge is weak – one student in two. These results basically confirm other studies that have been undertaken at the national and sub-regional levels.

With respect to the non-formal system, the data that would enable us to establish the level of basic knowledge are not available either at the national or at the sub-regional levels. It was therefore decided to carry out specific surveys, using a concept that is currently the subject of study at the international level: the degree of basic knowledge. The degree of basic knowledge takes into account many different levels of various skills (rather than a sole indicator that classifies learners as either literate or non-literate).

The results show that the year following the end of the first full cycle of literacy (AI + FCB), 7 out of 10 adults could be considered to be literate within the definition adopted by the UNESCO, whereas only 1 out of 2 could be regarded as having acquired skills within the meaning of the level of basic knowledge as defined in Dakar. There is a notable difference in the results when these are disaggregated by gender. Age, however, does not appear to play a significant role in achievement.

10 Approximate figures, not representative.
11 Idem.

ADAPTABILITY

3.3 Literacy of the population aged 10+ not currently or never being schooled

N: 1998

F	Urban		Rural		BF	
	M	**F**	**M**	**F**	**M**	**F**
10-14	3.4	3.3	4.4	2.8	4.3	2.8
15-24	6.9	5.5	6.9	4.1	6.9	4.2
25+	9.0	4.4	7.4	3.3	7.6	3.4
Total	**8.1**	**4.6**	**6.7**	**3.4**	**6.8**	**3.5**

At best every 4 years

3/ EP 98 (preferably EP 2003 as soon as it is available)

This indicator provides information on the capacity of the non-formal sector for basic education to provide education for all the population that does not have access to or has been excluded from the formal system. The threshold of age 10 corresponds to the age at which the child can no longer claim a right of access to schooling at the primary level.

This indicator enables an estimation of the contribution of non-formal education as part of the total level of literacy nation-wide. The results indicate that this contribution is significant, since the census showed that 5% represents approximately one quarter of the global level of literacy at the time of the survey, despite the non-formal sector never having consumed more than 1% of the public budget for education prior to the year 2000.

The main limitation of this indicator lies in the nature of the information relating to literacy levels gathered during census or demographic surveys. This information is based on data established according to the statements made by heads of households. These household heads often confused school attendance with literacy, and tended to under-estimate the achievement of literacy in their statements.

ADAPTABILITY

3.4 Evolution of GER with respect to GIR	**P:** Years | **00-01** **01-02** **02-03** **03-04** **F:** | 0.9 (+) 0.9 (+) 0.8 (+) 0.75 (+)	Annual	**2/** DEP/MEBA

This indicator measures the real progress accomplished in schooling. Associating the change in the gross rate of schooling (TBS) with the gross rate of enrolments (TBA), we can measure the actual change in the receptive capacity of the system at the primary school level. The TBS is too frequently presented as the key indicator for measuring access to school. The criticism that may be made in relation to this indicator – *save the fact that it relates more to the rate of enrolment than to the rate of schooling* – is that it often fails to describe the inertia of the school system. A better use of the TBS may be made in linking this indicator to the TBA which represents the number of students entering the first year with respect to the total number of 7 year old children. It thus becomes clear that a low rate of enrolment is a leading indicator of deterioration in the TBS. Where this does not hold true, it is generally due to the school system retaining students by *unnecessarily* forcing them to repeat a year. The qualitative dimension of the analysis can therefore be proxied by using these two, essentially quantitative indicators together.

As regards Burkina Faso, the choice made to use the gross rates can be explained, on the one hand, by the very weak rates of schooling and, on the other hand, by the important distinction that prevails between the net and the gross rates[12]. This choice also corresponds to the goal set in this regard by the PDDEB (TBS of 70% in 2010) and in the follow-up of the strategic framework for poverty reduction[13] (TBS for girls and TBS the most disadvantaged rural areas).

In Burkina Faso, the analysis of the change in the TBS with respect to the TBA over the past five years shows a strong correlation (from 0.9 to 0.75), which is the result of a positive dynamic. (see DT n° 8)

12 According to the figures presented in the intermediate report by the UNESCO on EFA, 7.8 % of primary pupils in Burkina Faso are ahead of the official age and 11.5% are behind the official school age (1999/2000), op. cit. p. 253.

13 Cadre stratégique de lutte contre la pauvreté (CSLP) / Strategic Poverty Reduction Framework

ADAPTABILITY

Indicator	Data	Frequency	Source
3.5 Examination pass rate (primary school certificate or literacy certificate)	See table below	Annual	**2/** DEC/MEBA

In %

Years	**00-01**	**01-02**	**02-03**	**03-04**
Province				
F/				
Male			77.1	82.6
Female			70.1	72.4
NF/				
Male	89.1	87.2	87.7	84.5
Female	76.9	77.2	78.3	
National				
F/				
Male			73.1	77.0
Female			66.1	69.6
NF/				
Male	73.7	80.6	85.7	
Female	80.7	77.9	77.5	

The pass rate for examinations, as an instrument for the final assessment of basic education cycles either formal or non-formal, is usually a good indicator of the internal efficiency of the system. It is also important from a social perspective.

The relevance of this indicator is sometimes questionable, owing to its “political” character: a slight reduction in the standard of the exam or in the instructions for its correction may cause considerable variation in the results. Some countries have been willing to manipulate results in this way.

In Burkina Faso, this indicator is part of the accepted goals of the PDDEB and plays a key role in evaluating the demand for access to higher education both formal and non-formal, that is, entry into secondary-level schooling and/or professional or vocational training. The qualitative interpretations of this indicator and its evolution over time deserve greater attention.

3.6 Primary school completion rate by gender	**P: in %**	Annual	**2/** DEP/MEBA

Years	**00-01**	**01-02**	**02-03**
Girls	18.5	19.1	20.9
Boys	26.6	26.3	28.3
Total	22.7	22.7	24.6

This indicator measures the relationship between the number of students in CM2 who do not need to repeat a year and the total number of children aged 12 (this corresponds to the age bracket in the final year of primary school). As with the gross rate of enrolment (in the first year), this indicator is a proxy for the gross rate of enrolment in the final year.

This indicator gives a first estimate of the contribution of the formal system to the future national literacy rate as far as those children who have reached the CM2 level may be regarded as being durably literate.

With a completion rate of 25% (20% for women), the formal system only contributed to a relatively minor increase in the literacy rate estimated at 21.8% in 2003, a level that is not sufficient to meet the target of 40% literacy for women and men by 2010.

ADAPTABILITY

4.1 Number of radio stations including basic education in their programming	**N: 2004** 14 radio stations	Annual	**3/** Board for Information (CSI)

This indicator is a measure of the system's dynamics, at least with respect to the non-formal sector. The programming of information relating to literacy by local radio stations often acts as a catalyst for the creation of literacy centres, and provides an important stimulus to the management committees of these centres. The indicator is also an undiscussed factor in the creation of demand for schooling and in the activities of parents' associations. In addition, radio stations perform an important role in the dissemination of information amongst populations where the majority of persons are illiterate.

Out of the 29 radio stations registered by the Board for Information (CSI) for the whole territory of Burkina Faso, 14 include programmes on basic education within their programming. These programmes are aimed, for the most part, at children, at teachers, and at parent-teachers. The programmes provide practical tips in relation to education (*fréquence mômes, espace enfants, rendez-vous des petits de l'école primaire, sac au dos*) and, some of them also give information on literacy (*antenne linguistique*).

It should be noted that not all the radio stations that exist in Burkina Faso are taken into account by the CSI. Only those radio stations that have sent up-to-date information including financial reports, a programming guide, and a detailed report on their staff are included in the census.

ADAPTABILITY

4.2 Percentage of literacy centres that organise reading and writing clubs	**P: 2003-2004** 36.3 %	Annual	**4/** Sanmatenga n= 245 centres

This indicator measures the number of centres that keep and develop instrumental knowledge through the organisation of reading and writing clubs either during the interval between two intensive courses or at the end of the whole learning cycle.

This indicator is linked to the question of the learning environment, which is an essential element in the capitalisation of acquired literacy and in its functionality. The enrichment of the learning environment is at the centre of the post-literacy activities promoted under the PDDEB.

The results at the provincial level indicate that approximately one third of centres take into account this dimension of literacy, in spite of the fact that this is not mentioned in any of the instructions from the authorities nor is it specifically funded by donors. This shows that it is possible to stimulate social dynamics through policies that are comprehensive and coherent in promoting post-literacy initiatives and a learning environment.

15. INDICATORS OF AVAILABILITY

<table>
<tr>
<td>1.1 Percentage of malnourished children by age cohort (proxy indicator of the health status for children aged 4)</td>
<td>N: 1998
<table><tr><td></td><td>Children aged 4 years</td></tr><tr><td>Chronic malnutrition (index height/age; -2 ET)</td><td>46 %</td></tr><tr><td>Severe growth retardation (index height/age; -3 ET)</td><td>19 %</td></tr></table></td>
<td>Depends on the data source</td>
<td>3/ EDSBF 1998</td>
</tr>
<tr>
<td colspan="4">This indicator is an estimation of the share of children for whom the right to adequate food is not met.
Owing to the lack of available data for children aged 7 years a proxy was used: the percentage of malnourished children aged 4. This indicator is regularly informed through demographic and health surveys.
For Burkina Faso, 46% of children aged 4 are malnourished and the hypothesis is that there is a similar level of malnutrition for children aged 7. This result shows in a striking manner the necessity of promoting non-formal pre-school education in an integrated approach (nutrition, health, and pre-school education in accordance with the Jomtien and Dakar conferences) and of promoting school nutrition (canteens). If real progress is to be made towards universal education, the needs of the poor and malnourished cohorts of the population must be taken into account.</td>
</tr>
</table>

AVAILABILITY

1.2 Net enrolment ratio for disabled and for non-disabled learners

N: Year 1996

	Urban			Rural			Total		
Dis.	**Boy**	**Girl**	**T**	**Boy**	**Girl**	**T**	**Boy**	**Girl**	**T**
No	52.3	44.0	48.1	14.0	6.2	10.2	16.5	8.8	12.7
Yes	14.3	28.6	21.4	7.1	3.7	5.8	7.4	5.4	6.6

10 years

3/ INSD (census 1996)

This indicator reveals the extent to which a medical disability is transformed into a social disability through the lack of respect for a fundamental human right: the right to primary education. It is a good measure of the level of discrimination or lack of discrimination as regards access to school.

The declarative nature of the disability during data collection almost certainly gives rise to an under-reporting of disabled children at school. This statistical bias does not mean, however, that the indicator is not relevant or that an analysis of the data is not worthwhile.

For Burkina Faso, the data clearly show that in all regions and for both genders, the population of disabled children is less likely to be schooled. The ratio is of 1 to 2 as compared with the non-disabled population. The promotion of the concept of the “integrating school” for non-severely disabled children and the promotion of specialised structures for other disabled children should form part of any plans related to the availability of education in pursuit of the goal of education for all.

AVAILABILITY

Indicator	Values	Frequency	Source
1.3 Percentage of teachers with public-owned housing in good condition	**P:** in %	Annual	**2/** DEP/MEBA

Years	**00-01**	**01-02**	**02-03**
F	37.4	45.2	42.5

This indicator measures the quality of teachers' living and working conditions. This is particularly crucial in rural settings. It is not a hidden measure of comfort, prestige or income.

In fact, the opportunities for keeping teachers in rural areas as well as the quality of their teaching partially depend on the existence of functional housing. This housing allows them to prepare their lessons effectively, to receive parents and students outside their classes, and, in a general manner, to play their social role in extra-curricular activities.

The results and field surveys have shown that more than half of the teachers do not have housing that meets minimum standards of adequacy. This situation partially explains the disappointing results of the educational system in rural areas.

AVAILABILITY

1.4 Percentage of trained teachers in primary education	**F:** in %	Annual	**2/** DEP/MEBA

Years	**00-01**	**01-02**	**02-03**
P	NA	NA	84,7
N	76.6	80.4	86.0

This indicator measures the share of teachers who obtained the minimum level of qualifications required within the formal sector.

In Burkina Faso, the minimal qualification required is the CEAP. Since 2003, the public sector has only recruited qualified teachers. In the private sector, however, teachers are still often recruited at the level of the BEPC. Teachers in French-Arabic schools do not have any system of professional training.

This system should change as the training provided in the National Schools for Primary-School Teachers (Ecoles Nationales des Enseignants du Primaire (ENEP)) does not automatically lead to employment in the public sector but rather gives graduates the opportunity to apply for a position in either the public or the private educational system. The managers of private schools therefore have a pool of qualified personnel available to take up teaching positions. Nevertheless, owing to the difficulties related to the adjustment from training to employment, it is likely that the transition will take some time.

AVAILABILITY

1.5	**F:**		
A/Annual participation of teachers in the training group **B/**Annual participation of teachers in educational conferences **C/**Annual participation of teachers in other forms of training	**A/** 94.6% (03-04) **B/** 84.0% (03-04) **C/** NA	Annual	**2/** DPEBA

These three indicators measure the actual level of participation of teachers in continuing education. The results of the first two indicators are very encouraging.

To interpret these data, one should note that participation in GAP (A) and educational conferences (B) is compulsory, at least in theory. It is important therefore to include other forms of continuing education. Even though the information is not currently available, the indicator is maintained. It is important to underline the need to strengthen continuing education as a result of the reduction of initial teacher training as foreseen in the framework of the PDDEB in Burkina Faso. The initial training of teachers will drop from two years to one.

In order to ensure the quality of education, it is imperative to strengthen initial teacher training through a variety of relevant continuing education options. Such options are currently lacking. The GAP attempt to meet those needs that are linked to the daily practice of teaching, but they do not meet needs in terms of training (appropriate subjects).

AVAILABILITY

Indicator	Data	Frequency	Source
1.6 Number of schools and literacy centres with respect to educational personnel (F) or supervisors (NF)	**P:**	Annual	**2/** DEP/MEBA, DGAENF **3/** FONAENF

Years	**00-01**	**01-02**	**02-03**
F	11	9	9
NF	NA	NA	5

This indicator provides information on the availability of training for basic educational structures (schools and centres). The results show that the ratios are satisfactory in Burkina Faso. The field surveys carried out showed, however, that the ratio of training was less problematic than the huge distances that must be travelled between different centres and schools.

In the formal sector, one of the problems raised in the surveys was that trainers were more focused on administrative tasks than on tasks related to learner support.

In the non-formal sector, we note that the number of supervisors[14] should be tied to the level of linguistic diversity and not only to the number of centres in the area. In practice, in order to provide results that meet a given standard of quality, operators who run literacy centres in several languages (for instance, jula, cerma or karaboro) will find themselves in a situation where they are required to organise and pay for supervisors who are competent in each of these languages.

14 Principal (IP), inspectors and educational counsellors.

AVAILABILITY

Indicator	Values	Frequency	Source
1.7 Number of classes where no teacher was available for at least two consecutive months during the year	**P:** Years / **02-03** / **03-04** **F** / 12 classes / 3 classes	Annual	**2/** DPEBA

This indicator gives information with regard to the capacity of the formal system to use its resources in teaching personnel. In the past, Burkina Faso has been through periods in which some classes were without a teacher for the whole school year[15]. The current results show that the measures taken to resolve this problem have been successful. There remains, however, the recurrent problem of the non-payment of salaries for new teachers, which creates serious problems of absenteeism at the start of each school year for those classes that are to be taught by new teachers, even if this situation does not appear in the statistics.

15 In principle, in these cases, the students concerned are not regarded as having repeated a year.

AVAILABILITY				
	2.1 Disbursement degree of promised funds	**NA**	At each stage of the PDDEB	**1/** SP/PDDEB, BPE

This indicator measures the actual degree of realisation of the goals established by the PDDEB with respect to the internal and external mobilisation of necessary funds. The calculation refers to the amount of funding that is considered to be necessary within the framework of the PDDEB, including specific measures and the goals related to the development of the system.

This indicator cannot be documented in a precise manner, but its general impact can be assessed. The interest of the indicator lies in its connection with the indicator on the rate of commitment of funding received (ind. 1.3, Adaptability), in order to observe the relationship between the capacities for resource mobilisation and the capacities for absorbing these resources. In this regard, it appears that in Burkina Faso the problem is particularly acute with respect to the formal sector's capacities for resource absorption.

AVAILABILITY

Indicator	Values	Periodicity	Sources
2.2 Equipment level of schools and literacy centres with regard to water, canteens, and toilets	see table P below	Annual	**2/** DEP/MEBA **3/** FONAENF, DGAENF **4/** n=245 centres

P:

Years	**00-01**	**01-02**	**02-03**	**03-04**
F				
Water	54.7	38.1	47.4	
Canteen	78.6	83.2	94.4	
Toilets	60.0	58.4	63.7	
NF				
Water				80.4
Canteen				59.0
Toilets				13.9

This indicator assesses the availability of the equipment which is deemed as necessary for schools and literacy centres with regard to sanitation, hygiene, availability of classroom facilities and the facilitation of the attendance of women and girls.

For the formal sector, there is a database that enables this indicator to be informed; this information is limited by the value of the data themselves, which are based on self-reporting, and by their representativeness. In practice, if a province is part of the "school canteen" programme, the result will be very positive. If, by contrast, this is not the case, the result will be nearly zero.

For the non-formal sector, in the absence of accessible data, the information and the results were obtained through surveys at the provincial level. The results are valid but not representative.

The availability of water in schools is a crucial problem, especially in a country where temperatures during lessons are between 30 and 45 degrees celsius for at least six months during the school year. The number of literacy centres that have toilets is very low, a situation which does not favour the participation of women and girls.

The progress being made in systems of statistical information should enable a better information base for this indicator at the relevant levels – the national level and at the provincial level, thereby allowing for comparative analyses between provinces with a view to investigation and action.

AVAILABILITY

2.3 Percentage of classrooms and literacy centres made from permanent materials and in good condition

P:

Years	**00-01**	**01-02**	**02-03**	**03-04**
F				
Solid walls	93.0	93.5	93.8	
Good walls	92.6	91.3	92.8	
Good roofs	91.2	90.3	90.8	
NF				
Perm. mat.				26.1
In good cond				60.4

Annual

2/ DEP/MEBA
3/ FONAENF, DGAENF
4/ n= 245 centres

This indicator measures the share of locations where basic educational activities take place in conditions that are acceptable from the point of view of requirements for learning, security, and social recognition.

The results indicate that, as a general rule, 90% of the schools in the formal system are in good condition. On the other hand, in the non-formal system, it would appear that only 6 literacy centres out of 10 have facilities that are in good condition. This indicator reveals that only about one quarter of the centres have been built with permanent materials (26%), while the majority are in buildings that were not designed for this purpose (most of the centres are located in borrowed premises). In other words, this data means that three quarters of literacy centres, which have been known as "permanent centres for literacy and training" since the 1990s, are not really considered as such by planners and officials.

AVAILABILITY

2.4 Percentage of classrooms and literacy centres with the necessary equipment (blackboards, tables, desks, chairs, with and without cupboards/cabinets/trunks)

P: in %

Years	**00-01**	**01-02**	**02-03**	**03-04**
F				
Necessary equipement	62.7	64.8	58.6	
+ cupboard	44.4	43.5	45.6	
NF				
Necessary equipement	NA	NA		93.9
+ cupboard	NA	NA		4.5

Annual

2/ DEP/MEBA
3/ FONAENF, DGAENF
4/ n= 245 centres

This indicator measures the share of premises dedicated to basic education that have the necessary equipment to enable them to function. The equipment that is considered as necessary by the DEP includes: blackboards, tables, benches, chairs, cupboards, or a trunk.

As the collection of these different elements requires a considerable amount of additional work on the data, it was decided that the pieces of equipment that make up the minimum standard are mutually exclusive. In this way, the lowest percentage was retained each time. Taking into account the differences that exist in the availability of a cupboard, it was decided that these figures should appear separately.

The results indicate that for the formal sector there is a serious lack of equipment, particularly with respect to cupboards; this means that teachers are responsible for keeping documents and teaching materials in their homes.

For the non-formal sector, the availability of benches and blackboards was widespread. However, there was a systematic lack of cupboards; this situation underlines the precariousness of the training which claims, in theory, to be permanent.

AVAILABILITY

<table>
<tr>
<td>2.5 Percentage of students and learners with textbooks for reading and mathematics</td>
<td>
P:
<table>
<tr><td>Years</td><td>00-01</td><td>01-02</td><td>02-03</td><td>03-04</td></tr>
<tr><td>F</td><td></td><td></td><td></td><td></td></tr>
<tr><td>Reading</td><td>54.3</td><td>42.3</td><td>48.0</td><td></td></tr>
<tr><td>Maths</td><td>39.6</td><td>33.8</td><td>76.4</td><td></td></tr>
<tr><td>NF</td><td></td><td></td><td></td><td></td></tr>
<tr><td></td><td>NA</td><td></td><td></td><td>94.7</td></tr>
</table>
</td>
<td>Depends on the data source</td>
<td>2/ DEP/MEBA
4/ n= 245 centres</td>
</tr>
</table>

This indicator measures the share of students and learners who have the minimum amount of learning materials at their disposal. Surveys enabled us to conclude that there is a significant gap, although this is difficult to measure, between the theoretical availability and the actual availability of these resources.

In the formal sector, the availability of textbooks was calculated for all the levels of schooling taken together. The PDDEB states that, in the end, each student should have a textbook. The joint missions for the evaluation and follow-up of the PDDEB showed, however, that serious difficulties exist with respect to the development/updating, printing, and distribution of books, and that these have yet to be resolved.

In the non-formal sector, the enrolment fees cover the cost of one textbook. The lack of textbooks is due to their under-production, which is a serious problem. It seems that the best results were obtained by those operators who took the initiative to make their own photocopies of the school material. In addition, it should be noted that textbooks and literacy guides in AT and in FCB are in the process of being modified, and that a new "editorial policy" is being elaborated.

AVAILABILITY

2.6 Indicator	Results	Frequency	Source
2.6 Percentage of literacy centres with access to a library or documentation centre	**P: Year 2004** **NF:** 10.2 %	At each stage of the PDDEB	**4/** n= 245 centres

As an addition to indicator 4.2 on the capacity of adaptation of proactive centres with respect to post-literacy and learning environments, this indicator measures the external supply in this field by way of libraries and resource centres.

The results are very weak (approximately 10%) and show that post-literacy and the encouragement of a learning environment are the "poor cousins" in the non-formal sector: the overwhelming majority of centres do not have external bookshelves or library cupboards. However, the achievement of the goals of the PDDEB pre-supposes a special effort in this area, which would stimulate demand for non-formal basic education.

AVAILABILITY

2.7 Percentage of literacy centres with a child-minding facility	**P: Year 2004** **NF:** 31.8 %	Annual	**4/** n= 245 centres

This indicator measures the internal spontaneous efforts made to care for pre-school aged children during the training of women. Despite the fact that there have been few clear policies or programmes in this area to date, the results may be viewed as very encouraging.

For Burkina Faso, the indicator shows that it is not unrealistic to seek to integrate organised activities for the education of pre-schoolers during the periods of child care that occur during literacy courses, training or other income-generating activities for women (which amount nearly to one thousand hours).

It should be noted that the terminology used does not imply that the structures for child care are permanent. These child-care facilities may exist in ad hoc spaces organised for the occasion, under the responsibility of women who have volunteered and have been accepted for this job. These women can benefit from specific training as regards the health and development of children aged under 7 years.

16. INDICATORS OF ACCESSIBILITY

Indicator	Values					Periodicity	Source / Sample
1.1.1 Percentage of women teachers and trainers	**P:** in %					Annual	**2/** DEP/MEBA **4/** n= 245 centres
	Years	**00-01**	**01-02**	**02-03**	**03-04**		
	F	21.3	22.9	25.4	32.3		
	NF	NA	NA	NA	33.9		

This indicator measures the share of women within the teaching staff in the formal sector as well as among instructors and trainers in the non-formal sector. The results show a very low share of women, although the trend is moving in a positive direction (one in four in the formal sector and one in three in the non-formal sector).

We note that constraints linked to women's employment represent a new difficulty with respect to education for women and young girls. Indeed, these constraints reinforce the physical and psychological obstacles that stand in the way of a full enjoyment of rights.

In the formal sector, it became evident during surveys that young women frequently suffered from gender discrimination during lessons, and that this discrimination had a negative impact on their schooling. Also, the low level of representation of female teachers (particularly in rural areas where they are extremely rare) is a key factor that discourages young girls from continuing their studies.

In the non-formal sector, surveys show that when the trainer was a woman, this had a positive impact on women's literacy.

ACCESSIBILITY

Indicator	Values	Frequency	Source
1.1.2 Female to male net primary enrolment ratio	**P:**	Annual	**2/** DEP/MEBA **3/** INSD

Years	**00-01**	**01-02**	**02-03**	**03-04**
F	0.6	0.6	0.59	0.61

This indicator measures the degree of inequality in access to school for girls with respect to boys. The equality index concerning the net rate of schooling (TNS) allows us to assess progress towards one of the main goals of EFA.

The results show that the index value is insufficient with regard to the goals fixed at the Dakar Forum. In addition, in light of the important differences that exist, it would be particularly interesting to disaggregate this indicator at the urban and rural levels.

ACCESSIBILITY

1.1.3 Female to male drop-out (NF) and abandonment (F) rate

P:

Years	**00-01**	**01-02**	**02-03**
F			
CP1	1.21	0.88	0.94
CP2	0.55	0.67	2.59
CE1	0.86	1.08	1.02
CE2	0.88	0.74	0.50
CM1	1.27	0.90	0.97
NF			
AI	1.33	1.33	1.76
FCB	1.50	1.35	1.30

Annual

2/ DEP/MEBA, DGAENF

This relationship measures discrimination at the level of school retention of girls and boys. While the indicator does not show a marked level of discrimination, it must be interpreted in the light of relatively new social phenomena: within cities, the school takes on the role of carer for children whose parents work; in rural areas, the lack of proximity of schools tends to increase the risk of non-enrolment and school abandonment of girls.

ACCESSIBILITY

As regards the rate of school drop-out, it must be reiterated that this indicator relates to the non-formal sector and that it also includes school failure. This distinction comes from the concentrated and short duration of the two phases of basic education: AI + FCB = between 600 and 800 hours. The result shows a high level of discrimination here. This situation can be explained primarily by the weight of social obligations for women, which means that they are often unable to attend school regularly. This then leads to failure and/or abandonment. During field surveys, it was observed that it was the combination of objective factors (real difficulties in achieving progress in learning) and psychological factors (coming back to the centre after an absence was seen as shameful, even if the reasons for the absence were justifiable) that often led women to abandon and/or fail. Unfortunately, the most useful means for remedying this situation (frequent revision, self-learning timetables for reading and writing, 'pairing' of students, and so on) are no longer being used.

<table>
<tr><td>1.2.1 Number of 2nd year basic literacy training centres (FCB) with respect to the number of 1st year basic literacy training centres (AI)</td><td>P:
<table><tr><th>Province</th><th>01-02</th><th>02-03</th><th>03-04</th></tr><tr><td>NF</td><td>0.48</td><td>0.75</td><td>0.51</td></tr></table></td><td>Annual</td><td>2/ DPEBA
3/ DGAENF</td></tr>
</table>

This indicator measures the opportunities offered to learners to complete the minimum educational requirements (AI + FCB), that constitute the core of the right to education and allow access to other forms of training and rights.

The results show that the number of FCB centres is much less than the number of AI centres. It should be noted that the FONAENF integrated this requirement into its policies and in its practices in connection with funding for literacy. For this reason, it is interesting to follow the progress of this ratio, which should, in principle, increase.

ACCESSIBILITY

Indicator	Values	Frequency	Source
1.2.2 Annual growth of the enrolment rate in 1st (AI) and in 2nd year (FCB) literacy training	**In %:** (see table below)	Annual	**2/** DEP/MEBA, DGAENF

In %:

NF	**02-03**	**03-04**
National		
AI	- 0.1	0.4
FCB	- 0.1	0.6
Province		
AI	- 0.5	3.4
FCB	- 0.2	2.1

This indicator is an indicator of progression. Its irregular assessment in Burkina Faso points to the necessity of a durable policy of maintenance of the funding obtained and of the mobilisation of new funding sources, to increase the number of students enrolled both in AI and in FCB. This requires adequate planning and communication in order to enable all those in AI to move on to FCB.

The FONAENF has committed itself to follow this difficult path with encouraging results that have been confirmed by the progression in the indicators that include current campaigns as well as those planned for the future.

ACCESSIBILITY				
	1.2.3 Percentage of the school-aged population located further than 2.5 km from a school	**NA**		**2/** Educational map (available for certain provinces only)

This indicator measures the share of the population that does not have access to formal basic education if we consider a school situated at more than 2.5 km away to be inaccessible within the territory of Burkina Faso (lack of means of individual or of collective transportation).

Unfortunately, there was no adequate information for this indicator. Production of this indicator requires that reference be made to an educational mapping tool that, for the time being, is only available for some provinces in Burkina Faso. This tool allows a census of the school-aged population within a radius of 2.5 km and to calculate thereby the rate of schooling of students nearby in the neighbourhood. This approach is the opposite of that taken in the classic school mapping process, which, at the administrative level, connects all those populations in the neighbourhood of a school without taking into consideration the distances that have to be travelled by the students (which could be up to 20 km, meaning therefore hours of walking or cycling). This situation is not compatible with effective schooling, unless within a boarding school context or unless the student is billeted out; both these options cannot be widely used and are, therefore not sustainable.

ACCESSIBILITY

Indicator	Values	Frequency	Source
1.2.4 Ratio of the gross enrolment rate in the capital city with respect to the province	**P:**	Annual	**2/** DEP/MEBA **3/** INSD

	00-01	**01-02**	**02-03**	**03-04**
F	3.23	3.24	2.89	2.74

The indicator measures the disparities between urban and rural areas. This indicator is difficult to produce as the delimitation between urban and rural zones has been the subject of controversy as well as different practices. Further, the urban area is steadily expanding. In addition, the fact that an area is considered as urban or rural does not represent a criterion for the establishment of districts for the purposes of basic education. For this reason, this indicator was only established at the provincial level, on the basis of a comparison of data between the provincial capital city (urban) and the rest of the province (rural). The stability of this division enables an analysis of the evolution of the relationship between the two zones. The different elements of the indicator show that schooling in a rural context is very behind schooling in an urban setting.

ACCESSIBILITY

1.3.1 Net rate of schooling (TNS) according to the family situation of the child

N: 1998

Family status	Urban			Rural			Burkina Faso		
	Boy	**Girl**	**Total**	**Boy**	**Girl**	**Total**	**Boy**	**Girl**	**Total**
Head of household's child	80.0	75.3	77.8	25.1	18.1	21.8	33.2	26.4	30.0
Other related children	72.8	59.3	65.4	32.2	15.3	23.9	36.7	21.1	28.9
Children who are not related	39.5	42.7	41.9	29.5	25.5	27.3	31.0	30.7	30.8
Total	78.3	70.7	74.6	26.8	17.5	22.3	34.0	25.2	29.8

Depends on the data source

3/ INSD (EP 2, 1998)

This indicator allows us to bring to light those inequalities in schooling related to the family status of children.

The data that enable us to clearly identify those children in situations of guardianship (confiage) are very rare. This family status may be included in the data through the family ties between children and the head of the household (CM). On the basis of available data, we can distinguish three categories of children: children of the CM, other related children, children who are not related; on the assumption that children in the care of guardians will fall within the latter two categories.

In light of the results of the 1998 survey, we should note the uncertainty of the information that appears in the following categories: guardianship for the purposes of schooling in rural areas and guardianship situations for work (notably domestic) in town and that mainly concern girls.

ACCESSIBILITY

1.3.2 Share of annual average cost of schooling with respect to total annual household expenditure[18]

N: Year 1998

Columns	Quintiles of total annual expenditure					Total
	1	**2**	**3**	**4**	**5**	
Urban	7.1	2.7	1.6	1.0	0.3	0.5
Rural	8.8	3.4	2.2	1.5	0.6	1.8
BF	8.7	3.4	2.1	1.4	0.4	1.3

Depends on the data source

3/ INSD (EP 2, 1998)

This indicator brings to the fore the burden of the minimum cost of schooling for children in household budgets if all of the school-aged children were at school. In this regard, it is one of the key indicators of the effective right to formal education for all, with no economic barriers to accessibility.

The median cost corresponds to the school fees for a child within the responsibility of the household times the average number of school-aged children. The expenses correspond to monetary expenditure and are shown by quintile. The average cost borne by households is calculated on the basis of the minimum package and the different contributions. For each class, the minimum package of school supplies is necessary for the student to start the school year. This package varies according to local conditions and takes into account the supplies that a student in a given class will need in order for her/him to attend lessons throughout the whole year. It is defined by the teachers. This means that the content of the package is not always the same for each class or for each teacher at the same level.

Concerning the results, we can note that it is in poor households and in those where there are the largest numbers of school-aged children that the cost is proportionately higher. This can be explained by the fact that there are more poor households in rural areas where the level of fertility is higher, where polygamous households are more common, and where households tend to have an extended family structure.

18 The average cost corresponds to the school fees for a child that are borne by the household multiplied by the average number of children of school age. The expenses correspond to monetary expenditure and are broken down by quintile. The average cost borne by households is calculated on the basis of the minimum package and different contributions. For each class, a minimum package of school supplies is necessary so that the student can begin the school year. The package varies according to the local situation and takes into account the supplies that a student in a given class must have in order to follow the course of studies under acceptable conditions for the whole year. It is defined by the teachers. This means that the content of the package is not always the same for each class or for each teacher at the same level (class).

ACCESSIBILITY

1.3.3 Share of annual average cost of literacy with respect to total annual household expenditure

N: 1998

	Quintiles of total annual expenditure					
Columns	**1**	**2**	**3**	**4**	**5**	Total
Urban	5.8	2.6	1.6	1.0	0.3	0.5
Rural	10.0	4.0	2.6	1.8	0.8	2.2
BF	9.8	3.9	2.4	1.6	0.6	1.5

Depends on the data source

3/ INSD (EP 2, 1998)

This indicator highlights the burden of the minimum cost of literacy/training for young people and adults on the family budget. In this regard, it is one of the key indicators of the effectiveness of the right to non-formal education for all, with no economic barriers to accessibility.

The median cost of literacy per household was estimated on the basis of information on the contributions of learners to their training in literacy. This estimate takes into account books and supplies that a learner requires to attend a literacy training course. The cost is evaluated at 3,650 Fcfa. On the basis of these cost estimates, the different costs were calculated using the same method as used for indicator 1.3.2. Here the population observed corresponds to those persons aged from 15 to 44 who are illiterate or who have never been to school.

As with formal schooling, it is in poor households that there are more people aged between 15 and 44 who are not literate or who have never been to school and, as a result, who have to make more efforts to achieve complete literacy. The burden of this cost is proportionately higher for those with lower incomes.

17. CONCLUSIONS

1/ The effectiveness of the right to education is not considered as an obligation of result but as a primary goal according to a programmatic view of rights. This theoretical bias gives rise to a practical bias whose main consequences are the failure to consider the variety of actors and their role in the implementation, respect for, and protection of the right to education. Yet, an important proportion of the commitments and activities in favour of basic education for all can be attributed to actors other than those States that have ratified the International Pact on Economic, Social, and Cultural Rights. The indicators may be considered as important instruments for providing information on and as forces for the development and legitimation of those activities that are undertaken by all relevant actors. The indicators show that the right to education continues to be considered as an ideal goal.

2/ The capacity or capability approach enables us to seize the multi-dimensional character of the right to education through the adoption of different perspectives for the observation. These different perspectives include not only those viewpoints related to the acceptability and accessibility of the system, that is, the existence of framework conditions that favour access to education for all, but also the availability and adaptability of the system that form the necessary resources for the development of basic knowledge. The scoreboard confirms that the means are not, in themselves, essential. It sheds light on important forms of discrimination with respect to the right to education, for example according to the family status of the child (in a situation of guardianship or not), gender, and the area of residence (urban or rural).

3/ The indicators underline the interactions between the four capacities in the scoreboard. These interactions appear notably in the difficulties encountered in putting some indicators within the scoreboard. This is the case, for example, for indicators 1.1 and 1.2, which relate to the health of learners and that were considered at the level of the availability of the system, while they could have just as easily been positioned at the level of accessibility. If health concerns above all the capacity of the system to respond, through available resources, to the specific needs of persons, this is in order to guarantee, in the end, the accessibility of the system to all without any form of discrimination. The indicator 3.3 on acceptability on the presence of income-generating activities for learners in literacy and training centres is also a good example of the linkages pointed out above. Income-generating activities for learners represent an acceptability issue as they provide a form of status recognition for adults, who are the target public for these programmes. It also raises the issue of the adaptability of the system in its response to the expectations of this public, for whom basic training represents an important opportunity cost.

4/ The indicators bring to light the connections between the right to education and other rights, in particular:

- *The right to information* (for example, all the indicators that were able to be informed and, in particular, indicator 4.1 on the adaptability of the system with respect to the number of radio stations that include basic education as part of their programming);
- *The right to food* (for instance, indicator 1.1 on availability with respect to malnourished children aged 4);
- *The right to health care* (for example indicator 3.4 on acceptability on schools that have a first-aid kit).

5/ The indicators confirm that **the effectiveness of the right to education comes up against major financial obstacles** that often prove insurmountable for the poorest families.

6/ The obligation of results is particularly important with respect to knowledge acquisition. In the formal sector, this obligation cannot be simply reduced to knowledge acquired at school, but must take into account relevant life skills (Jomtien, 1990). In the non-formal sector, the measure of the degree of basic knowledge is also necessary. In the case of Burkina Faso, this measure provides important results that avoid a simple distinction between those who claim to be literate and those who claim to be illiterate.

7/ It seems that rather than particular indicators, **groups of key indicators** are the most relevant:

A/ On **the appropriation of the right and the educational policies of the actors** (3 indicators):

Acceptability: indicators 2.4 and 2.7 on the involvement of actors in the definition, implementation, and evaluation of policies with respect to basic education;
indicator 3.5 on the existence of a functional framework for the expression of satisfaction of parents, teachers, and learners.

B/ On the **capacity for public financing in the system** (2 indicators):

Acceptability: indicators 2.1 and 2.2 on the contributions to basic education with respect to GDP. This group of indicators should be completed in the near future with the following two indicators provided for in the PDDEB:

Adaptability: indicator 1.3 on the commitment rate of funding;

Availability: indicator 2.1 on the disbursement degree of promised funding.

C/ On the **degree of coverage of fundamental educational needs** for all (8 indicators):

Adaptability: indicator 1.2 on the actual number of teaching hours;
indicator 2.4 on the proportion of children aged from 10 to 12 who have never been to school;

	indicator 3.2 on the level of basic knowledge;
	indicator 3.3 on the rate of literacy of the population aged 10 and over who are not or who have never been to school;
	indicator 3.1 and 3.6 on the rates of abandonment, drop out, and completion;
	indicator 4.2 on the percentage of literacy centres that organise reading or writing clubs.
Accessibility:	indicator 1.3.1 TNS according to the family status of the child.

D/ On **conditions of access to, teaching in and receptivity of the system** (9 indicators):

Adaptability:	indicator 2.1 percentage of learners enrolled in innovative educational programmes.
Acceptability:	indicator 3.3 on literacy centres that offer income-generating activities;
Availability:	indicator 1.1 on the health of children;
	indicator 1.3 on teacher housing;
	indicator 2.2 on school facilities such as water, toilets and canteens;
	indicator 2.5 percentage of students and learners who have textbooks for reading and mathematics;
	indicator 2.7 on literacy centres that have a structure for the care of preschool children.
Accessibility:	indicators 1.3.2 and 1.3.3 on the minimum cost of school and literacy borne by households.

8/ As a whole, **the indicators on the right to education bring to light both positive and negative dynamics** in connection with the policies for basic education that have been put into practice. With respect to positive dynamics, we notice an improvement in the equality between girls and boys through the net rate of schooling over the last three school years. In the non-formal sector, we observe a high rate of achievement (indicator 3.5, Adaptability) as well as a positive rate of growth in the numbers of AI and FCB during the last campaign (indicator 1.2.2, Accessibility). The growth in public funding must also be highlighted. The negative dynamics come to light in a marked way through disaggregated data. For example, one can observe inequalities of treatment according to the family status of the child. In urban areas, a girl under guardianship has much less chance of going to school than a girl who is not in a situation of guardianship (indicator 1.3.1, Accessibility).

9/ The approach that privileges data from the formal and non-formal basic education sectors is correct as regards the right to education. This approach allows us to measure the degree of effectiveness of the right to education for the province of Sanmatenga. The general conclusions that come out of the study are that for the formal sector, a lack of adaptability of the system gives rise to problems as regards the management of the means at the system's disposal. As for the non-formal sector, the indicators enabled us, for the first time, to measure the activities of different actors in connection with the non-school population whose educational needs have not been met. The strengths and the weaknesses of the non-formal sector are therefore brought to light, enabling us to dismantle a number of preconceived ideas (for instance, adaptability: indicator of to the level of achievement of the literacy certificate (high), indicator 4.2 on the percentage of literacy centres that organise reading or writing clubs (high); availability: indicator 2.3 on the percentage of literacy centres built with permanent materials (weak), indicator 2.7 on structures for the care of pre-school children (high); accessibility: indicator 1.1.3, relation between level of drop-out man/woman (unequal), and so on).

10/ The indicators bring to the fore the issue of the education of girls and women. This issue is key for development and for the fight against poverty. Progress in this area is the responsibility of all actors, both public and private. Implementation strategies cannot be the same for girls, on the one hand (role of reception conditions and teaching methods), and for women, on the other hand (emphasis on child care facilities, and on income-generating activities).

11/ Finally, the scoreboard on the right to education is **a tool for observation, for policy-making and for training**. In this respect, it represents a relevant basis for the creation of an observatory. The main tasks of this observatory should be to ensure the availability of data sources, their accessibility and their interpretation. Its role in terms of follow-up and analysis of data should occur in close cooperation with the goals of the PDDEB and the CSLP. The membership of the observatory should be open to researchers and actors working with basic education in the formal and non-formal sectors.

BIBLIOGRAPHY

- ***Monographs:***

CLING J.-P., RAZAFINDRAKOTO M., ROUBAUD F. (éds.) [2002], *Les nouvelles stratégies internationales de lutte contre la pauvreté*, Ed. DIAL/Ed. Economica

CONFEMEN (Conférence des ministres de l'éducation des pays ayant le français en partage) [1999], *Les facteurs de l'efficacité dans l'enseignement primaire: les Results du programme PASEC sur neuf pays d'Afrique et de l'Océan indien*, Rapport de synthèse du Programme d'Analyse des Systèmes Educatifs de la CONFEMEN (PASEC), Dakar

FRIBOULET J.-J., MEYER-BISCH P., LIECHTI V. (éds.) [2000], *Les Indicateurs du droit à l'éducation. La mesure d'un droit culturel, facteur de développement*, Commission suisse de l'UNESCO, IIEDH, Fribourg, Berne

MICHAELOWA Katharina [2000], *Dépenses d'éducation, qualité de l'éducation et pauvreté: l'exemple de cinq pays d'Afrique francophone*, documents techniques no. 157, Centre de développement de l'OCDE

OCDE [2001], *Du bien-être des nations: le rôle du capital humain et social. Enseignement et compétences*, Centre pour la recherche et l'innovation dans l'enseignement, OCDE, Paris

OCDE [2003], *Regards sur l'éducation. Les indicateurs de l'OCDE*, OCDE, Paris

PNUD [2000], *Rapport mondial sur le développement humain 2000. Droits de l'homme et développement humain*, De Boeck Université, Paris, Bruxelles

PNUD [2002], *Rapport mondial sur le développement humain: approfondir la démocratie dans un monde fragmenté*, De Boeck Université, Paris, Bruxelles

PNUD [2003], *Rapport mondial sur le développement humain: Les objectifs du Millénaire pour le développement: un pacte entre les pays pour vaincre la pauvreté humaine*, Economica, Paris

PNUD [2004], *Rapport mondial sur le développement humain: Liberté culturelle dans un monde diversifié*, Economica, Paris

UNESCO [2000a], *Rapport mondial sur l'éducation: Le droit à l'éducation. Vers l'éducation pour tous, tout au long de la vie*, UNESCO, Paris

UNESCO [2000b], *Statistical Document: Education for All, 2000 Assessment*, World Education Forum, 26-28 April 2000, Dakar, Senegal

UNESCO [2000c], *Rapport mondial sur la culture. Diversité culturelle, conflit et pluralisme*, Editions UNESCO, Paris

UNESCO [2002], *Education pour tous. Le monde est-il sur la bonne voie?*, Rapport mondial de suivi sur l'éducation pour tous, Ed. UNESCO, France

UNESCO [2003], *Déclaration universelle sur la diversité culturelle*, Série diversité culturelle n°1, éd. UNESCO, Paris

SEN Amartya [2000], *Un nouveau modèle économique: développement, justice, liberté*, Editions Odile Jacob, Paris

- ***Working papers, texts and official documents***

Association pour la Promotion de l'Education Non Formelle (APENF) [1999], *Etat des lieux de l'éducation non formelle au Burkina*, publié par l'Association pour la Promotion de l'Education en Afrique (ADEA), Ouagadougou

Association pour la Promotion de l'Education Non Formelle (APENF) [2000], *Etude d'impact de quinze programmes d'éducation de base non formelle au Burkina Faso*, publiée par l'Association pour la Promotion de l'Education en Afrique (ADEA), Ouagadougou

Comité des droits économiques sociaux et culturels (CESC) [1999], *Commentaire général concernant le droit à l'éducation* (Art.13): 08/12/99 E/C.12/1999/10, Pacte international relatif aux droits économiques sociaux et culturels, Vingt et unième session, 15 novembre - 3 décembre 1999, Genève

UNESCO [2000], *Education pour Tous: tenir nos engagements collectifs*, Forum mondial sur l'éducation, Dakar

Institut des sciences des sociétés (INSS), Institut de recherche pour le développement (IRD), Unité d'enseignement et de recherche en démographie (UERD) [2003], *Les cours du soir à Ouagadougou. Etude exploratoire*, Tome 1, Rapport, Ouagadougou

Institut interdisciplinaire d'éthique et des droits de l'homme (IIEDH) [2003], *Mesurer un droit de l'homme? L'effectivité du droit à l'éducation I. Enjeux et méthodes*, LIECHTI V., MEYER-BISCH P. (éds.), document de travail DT n° 7, IIEDH, Fribourg

Institut interdisciplinaire d'éthique et des droits de l'homme (IIEDH) [2003], *Mesurer un droit de l'homme? L'effectivité du droit à l'éducation II. Enquêtes*, FRIBOULET J.-J., LIECHTI V. (éds.), document de travail DT n° 8, IIEDH, Fribourg

Institut interdisciplinaire d'éthique et des droits de l'homme (IIEDH) [2003], *Mesurer un droit de l'homme? L'effectivité du droit à l'éducation III. Premiers Results et synthèse*, LIECHTI V. (éd.), document de travail DT n° 9, IIEDH, Fribourg

UNESCO, [1990], *Déclaration mondiale sur l'éducation pour tous: Répondre aux besoins éducatifs fondamentaux*, Jomtien

Ministère de l'enseignement de base et de l'alphabétisation (MEBA) [1996], *Loi d'Orientation de l'éducation du Burkina Faso*, Burkina Faso, Ouagadougou

Ministère de l'enseignement de base et de l'alphabétisation (MEBA) [1999], *Plan Décennal de Développement de l'Education de Base 2001-2010* (PDDEB), Burkina Faso, Ouagadougou

Ministère de l'enseignement de base et de l'alphabétisation (MEBA) [2004], *Rapport semestriel du Plan Décennal de Développement de l'Education de Base* (PDDEB) 01 juillet – 31 décembre 2003, 3e rapport, février 2004, Burkina Faso, Ouagadougou

ANNEXES

1/ DATA SOURCES

• Official sources

- Constitution of Burkina Faso (Law no. 002/97/ADP of 27 January 1997)
- Loi d'orientation de l'éducation N° 013/96 (Education Law)
- Secrétariat permanent du plan décennal de développement de l'éducation de base (Permanent Secretariat of the Plan for the Decade of the Development of Basic Education)
- Secrétariat permanent des ONG (Permanent NGO Secretariat)
- Direction du budget du Ministère des finances (Directorate for budget in the Ministry of Finance)
  Cadre stratégique de lutte contre la pauvreté (Strategic poverty-reduction framework)
  Bureau des projets d'éducation (Bureau for educational projects)

• Educational statistics

- Direction générale de l'alphabétisation et de l'éducation non formelle (General Directorate for literacy and non-formal education)
- Direction de la recherche documentaire et pédagogique (ex-IPB) (Directorate for documentary and educational research)
- Direction examens et concours (Directorate for examinations)
- Ministère de l'éducation de base et de l'alphabétisation (Ministry for Basic Education and Literacy)
  Direction des études et de la planification (Directorate for studies and planning)
  Direction des ressources humaines (Directorate for human resources)
  Direction générale de l'éducation de base (General Directorate for basic education)
  Direction des affaires financières (Directorate for financial affairs)
  Direction de l'allocation des moyens spécifiques aux écoles (Directorate for the allocation of specific budget to schools)
- Direction provinciale de l'enseignement de base et de l'alphabétisation (Provincial Directorate for Basic Teaching and Literacy)
  Circonscription de l'éducation de base (District for basic education)
- Institut national d'éducation de base non formelle (ex-INA) (National Institute for non-formal basic education)

• Non-scholastic statistics

- Institut national de la statistique et de la démographie (National Institute for Statistics and Demography)

Recensement général de la population et de l'habitation (1996) (General Census of population and living conditions)
Enquête démographique et de santé du Burkina Faso (1993/ 1998-99) (Demographic and health survey for Burkina Faso)
Enquêtes prioritaires sur les conditions de vie des ménages (1994-95/1998) (Priority surveys on household living conditions)

- Fonds pour l'alphabétisation et l'éducation non formelle (Fund for literacy and non-formal education)
- Cadre de concertation des ONG en éducation de base (NGO associative framework on basic education)
- Etudes spécifiques (ex. DT n° 9, PASEC, INSS, UERD, PAM - Programme alimentaire mondial, etc.) (Specific studies e.g. DT no. 9, PASEC, INSS, UERD, WFP – World Food Programme etc.)
- Partenaires techniques et financiers (programme alpha/formation de la coopération suisse, projet luxembourgeois, programme national de gestion des terroirs (PNGT)) (Technical and financial partnerships – Swiss cooperation programme on literacy/training, Luxembourg's programme, national programme for land management)
- Oeuvre suisse d'entraide ouvrière (OSEO) (Swiss Workers' Aid Society)

- **Surveys**

  - Surveys in the Provence of Sanmatenga

2/ LIST OF INDICATORS DISCARDED

ACCEPTABILITY

2.8 Percentage of literacy centres created and run by the communities.

Reason: this indicator is not relevant for Burkina Faso.

ADAPTABILITY

1.3 Percentage of teachers and trainers who adapt their curriculum to meet the expectations and needs spelt out by the learners.

Reason: this method of calculating the indicator has yet to be defined. It remains relevant.

2.5 Percentage of literate students attending or having attended technical or specific training or other forms of post-literacy education during the last three years.

Reason: this indicator is very interesting and relevant but its method of calculation is difficult.

4.2 Evolution of the copy run of the written press (number and extent of coverage).

Reason: information not available.

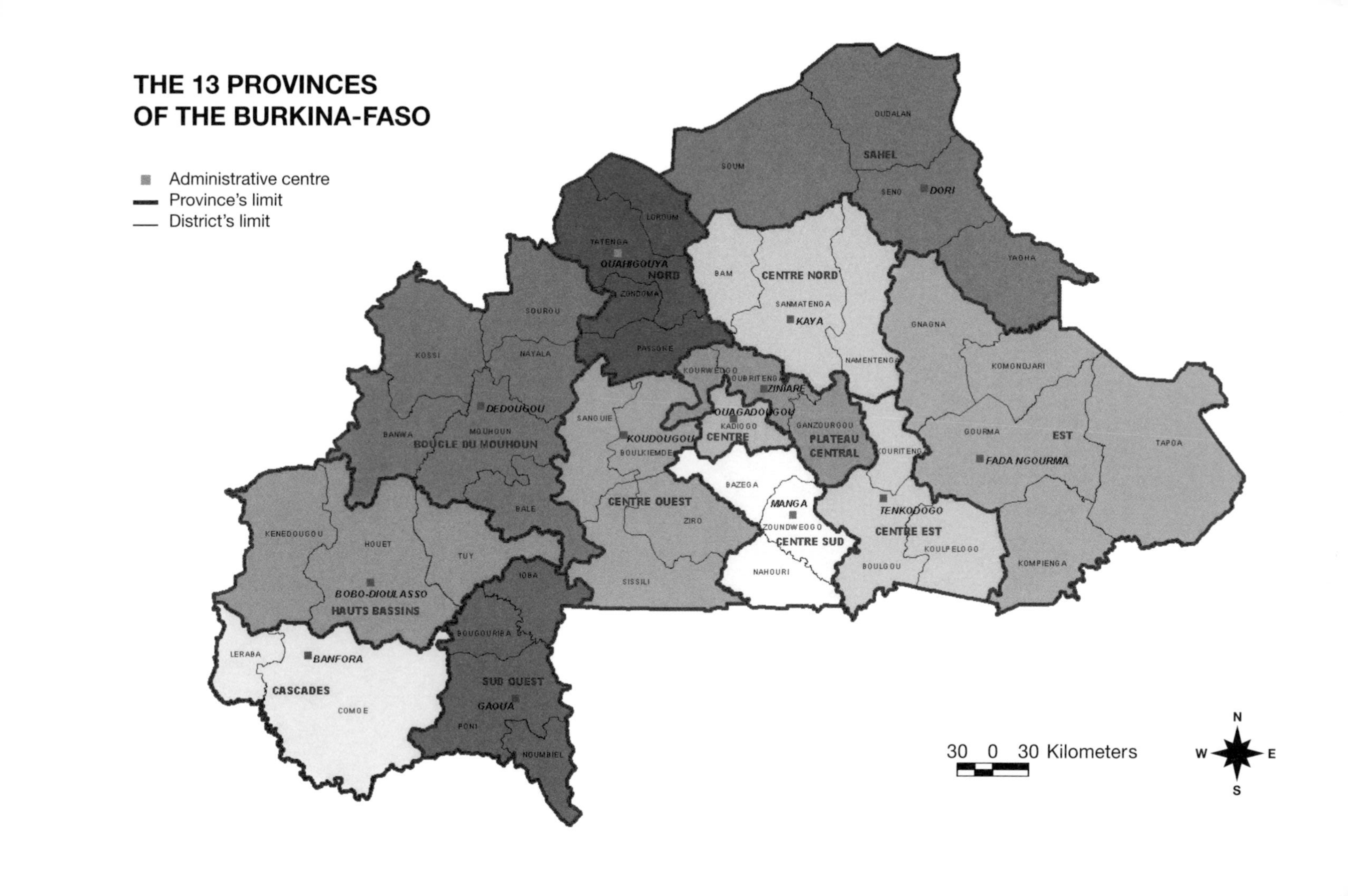
THE 13 PROVINCES
OF THE BURKINA-FASO
Administrative centre
Province's limit
District's limit
OUDALAN
SAHEL
SOUM
SENO
DORI
LOROUM
YATENGA
OUAHIGOUYA
NORD
ZONDOMA
PASSORE
YAGHA
BAM
CENTRE NORD
SANMATENGA
KAYA
NAMENTENGA
GNAGNA
KOMONDJARI
SOUROU
KOSSI
NAYALA
DEDOUGOU
BANWA
MOUHOUN
BOUCLE DU MOUHOUN
KOURWEOGO
OUBRITENGA
ZINIARE
OUAGADOUGOU
KADIOGO
CENTRE
GANZOURGOU
PLATEAU
CENTRAL
SANGUIE
KOUDOUGOU
BOULKIEMDE
KOURITENGA
GOURMA
EST
FADA NGOURMA
TAPOA
BAZEGA
MANGA
ZOUNDWEOGO
CENTRE SUD
NAHOURI
CENTRE OUEST
ZIRO
SISSILI
TENKODOGO
CENTRE EST
KOULPELOGO
BOULGOU
KOMPIENGA
BALE
KENEDOUGOU
HOUET
TUY
BOBO-DIOULASSO
HAUTS BASSINS
IOBA
BOUGOURIBA
LERABA
BANFORA
CASCADES
COMOE
SUD OUEST
GAOUA
PONI
NOUMBIEL
30 0 30 Kilometers
N
W
E
S